MIND AID PITARA

*A Self-Help Guide
to the Mysteries of your Mind...*

DR SMITA KAMAT GHOSH

ISBN
Paperback 979-8-89699-961-4
Hardcase 979-8-89744-636-0

Contents

Acknowledgement

Having an idea and turning it into a book is harder than I ever imagined, yet infinitely more rewarding than I could have hoped. The process has been both an internal challenge—requiring self-reflection and perseverance—and a deeply fulfilling journey.

This endeavor would not have been possible without the unwavering support and encouragement of my family, who stood by me at every step. I extend heartfelt gratitude to my friends, mentor, and guide for their belief in me and their vital contributions that helped bring this book to life.

Most importantly, I want to express my appreciation to **everyone** who stayed positive and inspired me to pursue my dream. Your motivation and faith have transformed an idea into *Mind Aid Pitara*, a resource I hope will guide and uplift others on their journey to better mental and emotional well-being. Thank you for being part of this accomplishment.

Foreword

Dr Smita Kamat Ghosh is the indie author of *Mind-Aid Pitara* and *Decoding Mithya*. By profession, she is a Research Psychologist, Research Mentor, Content Writer, and Soft Skill & Life Purpose Coach. With unwavering faith and determination, she envisions removing the stigma and shame surrounding mental health while fostering awareness and understanding.

Her journey as an author began with *Decoding Mithya*, where she skillfully dismantled societal myths about womanhood through a blend of storytelling and introspection. With *Mind-Aid Pitara*, she furthers her mission to support children, youth, and adults, offering them practical tools to break free from degrading mental and psychological health challenges.

Through her work, Dr. Smita aims to empower individuals to embrace their emotional well-being and live fuller, healthier lives.

Mind Aid Pitara: A Journey to Emotional Wellness

In a world where emotional well-being often takes a backseat, *Mind Aid Pitara* offers a compassionate guide to navigating life's psychological challenges. Written by Dr Smita Kamat Ghosh, a seasoned psychologist and counselor, this e-book provides practical tools, insightful advice, and accessible strategies to foster mental wellness.

With a focus on breaking the stigma surrounding mental health, *Mind Aid Pitara* is designed to empower individuals to understand their emotions, cope with stress, and develop healthy habits for a balanced life. Whether you're struggling with everyday pressures or seeking ways to boost your resilience, this book serves as a supportive companion on your journey toward emotional strength.

Packed with relatable examples, real-life scenarios, and easy-to-follow exercises, *Mind Aid Pitara* encourages readers to embrace their feelings, challenge negative thought patterns, and build a healthier mindset. Step into the world of emotional well-being, and unlock the tools to live with greater confidence and peace of mind.

Dr Smita Kamat Ghosh – Author Bio

Dr Smita Kamat Ghosh is a renowned psychologist, counselor, and author with a profound passion for empowering individuals, particularly women and girls, to unlock their full potential. With over a decade of experience in the field, Dr. Smita has worked extensively on mental health, women's empowerment, financial literacy, and youth mentoring. She is the author of *Safe Teen Steps*, a groundbreaking book that addresses the issues of sexting and pornography, and *Decoding Mithya*, a reflective exploration of the myths surrounding womanhood.

As a multilingual professional, fluent in English, Hindi, Marathi, Konkani, Bangla, and Gujarati, Dr. Smita has connected with diverse communities through her work, making her insights accessible to people from various backgrounds. She has been recognized for her contribution to the field of mental health and was honored with the National Level Best Counsellor Award by the Indian School Psychology Association in 2022.

Dr. Smita is also a sought-after speaker and consultant, having worked with organizations like UNESCO, where she shared her expertise on inclusion and diversity. Her work as an impact assessment consultant has taken her to over 150 villages, where she has helped uplift communities by providing psychological support and building awareness.

In addition to her clinical work, Dr. Smita is pursuing a Senior Management Program at IIM and has completed a course in public policy analysis from the London School of Economics. Her approach to mental health is grounded in the belief that emotional well-being is essential for a fulfilling life, and she is dedicated to breaking the stigma surrounding mental health through accessible resources like *Mind Aid Pitara*, her latest e-book.

Books by Dr Smita Kamat Ghosh

1. *Safe Teen Steps* **– Navigating the Digital Maze**

In today's world, teenagers are constantly exposed to the complexities of the digital age. *Safe Teen Steps* serves as a compass for young minds, guiding them through the labyrinth of sexting, pornography, and online safety. Through insightful advice, relatable case studies, and practical strategies, Dr Smita Kamat Ghosh empowers teens and parents alike to understand the risks, develop healthy boundaries, and foster a safe digital presence. This book is not just a guide; it's a call to action, encouraging teens to take control of their digital lives with confidence, responsibility, and respect for themselves and others.

2. *Decoding Mithya* **– In the Silence, We Find Our Voice**

In *Decoding Mithya*, Dr Smita Kamat Ghosh delves into the myths and misconceptions that have long defined womanhood. With a blend of storytelling, introspective questions, and philosophical reflections, the book challenges ingrained societal norms and invites readers to reimagine what it means to be a woman in the modern world. From the stereotypes of color-coded gender roles to the hidden stigmas of menstruation, Dr. Smita weaves a narrative that empowers women to break free from the chains of societal expectations. Through the eyes of Sakhi, the narrator, *Decoding Mithya* guides readers on a journey of self-discovery, offering both a mirror and a roadmap for redefining womanhood on their own terms.

3. ***Mind Aid Pitara*** **– Unlocking the Secrets to Emotional Wellness**

Mind Aid Pitara is more than just a book; it's a toolbox for mental well-being. Dr Smita Kamat Ghosh brings together her expertise as a psychologist and counselor to provide practical, actionable advice for navigating life's emotional challenges. With easy-to-follow exercises, real-life examples, and psychological insights, this book helps readers cultivate emotional resilience, manage stress, and foster mental strength. *Mind Aid Pitara* is an invitation to take control of your emotional health and embark on a journey of self-care, empowerment, and lasting peace of mind. Through its accessible approach, it challenges the stigma surrounding mental health and encourages readers to embrace their emotions as a path to healing and growth.

Preface

As the author of *Decoding Mithya,* a book that peels back the layers of societal myths around womanhood, I've witnessed how deeply misconceptions can impact our lives—not just socially, but emotionally and mentally as well. Our minds, much like our identities, are shaped by what we absorb from the world around us. Yet, mental health remains a topic shrouded in silence, cloaked by stigma and held captive by pervasive myths.

In India, this silence can be deafening. Conversations about mental health are often met with discomfort or dismissal. And while the realities of stress, anxiety, and emotional overwhelm touch each of us—regardless of age, caste, or gender—few feel equipped to navigate them. It is this gap that I aim to bridge with *Mind Aid Pitara.*

This psychological self-help guide is a curated collection of practical tools, designed to provide psychological first aid for the minor yet impactful crises of daily life. Much like a *pitara*—a treasure chest filled with essentials—this book offers simple, effective strategies to handle emotions like guilt, jealousy, failure, and negativity. These are not just issues to address but opportunities to build emotional resilience and rediscover self-worth.

Just as *Decoding Mithya* encouraged readers to challenge societal norms, *Mind Aid Pitara* invites you to decode your emotional patterns and take proactive steps toward mental wellness. Coping with life's pressures may seem daunting, but with the right tools, it is not just possible—it's empowering.

I hope this book serves as a guide, a friend, and a gentle nudge toward understanding yourself better. And as you journey through its pages, may you find the courage to break not just societal myths but also those within your own mind.

Warm regards,

Dr Smita Kamat Ghosh
Author of *Decoding Mithya*

Disclaimer for Mind Aid Pitara

Educational Purpose Only

Mind Aid Pitara is intended as a general resource to provide information and self-help tips for mental and emotional well-being. It does not constitute professional medical or psychological advice, diagnosis, or treatment.

Not a Substitute for Professional Help

The content within Mind Aid Pitara should never replace or delay the need for professional assessment, therapy, or intervention. If you are experiencing severe distress, suicidal thoughts, or any other urgent mental health concern, please seek immediate professional help from a licensed mental health practitioner, crisis helpline, or medical facility.

Individual Differences

Each person's mental health needs and experiences are unique. The techniques, activities, and suggestions provided may not be suitable for everyone. It is essential to use your judgment and adapt any strategy to your personal situation or consult with a qualified professional.

No Warranty or Guarantee

Although care has been taken to ensure that the information in Mind Aid Pitara is accurate and up to date, the author and publisher make no warranties or guarantees of any kind regarding its completeness, reliability, or suitability for your specific needs. Any action you take based on the information is strictly at your own risk.

Seek Appropriate Care

If you have any concerns or questions about your mental health, please consult a physician, therapist, or mental health professional. Never disregard or delay seeking professional advice because of information you have read in Mind Aid Pitara.

Chapter 1

Overview of the Pitara

As I journeyed through the writing of *Decoding Mithya*, uncovering the myths that society wraps around womanhood, one realization stood out: these societal constructs not only shape our identities but deeply influence our mental well-being. Much like the societal norms we challenge, mental health too carries its own stigma, leaving countless individuals grappling with the silence of unspoken struggles. *Mind Aid Pitara* was born out of a desire to break this silence and to offer a roadmap for nurturing our minds with care and intention.

The aim of *Mind Aid Pitara* is simple yet profound: to equip you with tools to create a healthier mindset, nurture and understand yourself, stabilize your personal energy, cultivate empathy, and practice positive thinking. It's a guide to help you rediscover balance in a world that often tilts us off course.

Aim of Mind-Aid Pitara

As we move through life, we often forget that our mental and emotional well-being requires just as much attention as our physical health. Our thoughts, emotions, and perceptions shape the world around us, but without the right tools, they can easily be overshadowed by stress, negativity, and self-doubt.

Mind-Aid Pitara is designed to provide those tools. It is a psychological self-help guide that serves as a treasure chest of practical, easy-to-follow tips and activities to help manage everyday mental and emotional struggles. Whether it's the weight of failure, guilt, jealousy, or simply the unrelenting pressure of life, this book aims to offer relief and a way forward.

The activities and insights in this book are built with one core goal in mind: to **create a healthier mindset**. But beyond just that, the *Mind-Aid Pitara* is here to:

- **Nurture and Understand the Self**: Cultivate self-awareness to embrace the full spectrum of your emotions and experiences.

- **Stabilize Personal Energy**: Learn to replenish yourself mentally, emotionally, and physically to stay grounded and strong.

- **Cultivate Empathy**: Build deeper understanding and compassion towards others, as well as yourself.

- **Practice Positive Thinking**: Develop the skills to shift your mindset towards growth, possibility, and optimism.

Understanding Mental Health & Mental Illness

Mental Health is not merely the absence of illness. It is a state of well-being that allows individuals to realize their potential, cope with the normal stresses of life, work productively, and contribute to their communities. It involves our emotions, our psychological state, and our ability to form positive relationships with others. Mental health isn't fixed—it's something that requires ongoing attention and care, just like physical health.

The World Health Organization defines mental health as:

- **Enjoying life**

- **Bouncing back from stress or sadness**

- **Setting and fulfilling personal goals**

- **Building and maintaining relationships**

Mental health is also intrinsically linked to cultural understandings, and as such, the definitions may vary. However, at its core, it is a holistic state of emotional and psychological well-being that nurtures a thriving individual.

Mental Illness

On the flip side, **mental illness** refers to health conditions involving changes in emotion, thinking, or behavior—or a combination of all three. These changes are often distressing and can significantly impair a person's ability to function socially, at work, or within the family.

Contrary to common misconceptions, mental illness is **common**. In fact, the National Institute of Mental Health reports that nearly one in five adults experience a mental illness in any given year. The key is to identify it early and take proactive steps to address it.

Influences on Mental Health and Wellbeing

Mental health doesn't exist in a vacuum. It is shaped by a range of **biological, psychological, social, and environmental factors**, which interact with each other in complex ways. These factors include:

- **Structural Factors**: Access to safe living environments, education, freedom from discrimination, and economic resources.

- **Community Factors**: A sense of belonging, social support, and involvement in community activities.

- **Individual Factors**: Self-management of emotions, communication skills, and personal coping mechanisms.

Together, these factors create a unique landscape of mental health that can either promote well-being or lead to distress, depending on how they are managed.

Stigma & Misconception - Mental Health

In many cultures, especially in India, mental health has been shrouded in stigma. The phrase **"Lok Kya Kahenge"** (What will people say?) captures the fear many individuals feel when it comes to discussing or seeking help for mental health issues. The social pressure to appear "normal" often overrides the need for self-care.

Mental health stigma manifests in various ways:

- **Fearing the label of 'madness'**: The idea that seeking help means you are weak or crazy.

- **The shame of being judged**: A fear of others' reactions or perceptions about one's struggles.

- **Family pressures**: Concerns about protecting "family honor" or avoiding shame that mental health struggles might bring.

This stigma is pervasive across caste, gender, age, and socio-economic status, preventing many from seeking help. The pressure to fit into societal norms often stops individuals from reaching out, leading to prolonged suffering.

Peel off the Stigma - Let's Talk About Mental Health

It's time to challenge the status quo. The *Mind-Aid Pitara* is here to break down these barriers and offer a safe space for understanding and addressing mental health. The journey begins with **self-reflection**, **empathy**, and **open conversations**. It's about understanding that mental health is not a weakness but an integral part of who we are.

Understanding Self-Administered First Aid

Just as we use first aid for physical injuries, the same proactive approach can be used for emotional and mental injuries. The *Mind-Aid Pitara* is filled with techniques and exercises to serve as your **mental health first aid kit**, ready to be used whenever necessary. These exercises provide immediate relief for the mental strains of daily life, empowering you to regain control and find peace in moments of turmoil.

- **What is Physical First Aid?**
    - Physical first aid involves basic steps like cleaning wounds, applying bandages, and offering initial treatment for minor injuries.

- **What is Mental Health First Aid?**
    - Similarly, mental health first aid involves using simple strategies to deal with emotional stress, anger, anxiety, or feelings of inadequacy.

The Art of Self-Care with Mind Aid Pitara

Self-care begins with understanding your unique needs. It's not a one-size-fits-all solution but a journey of discovering what works best for you. Whether it's journaling, mindfulness, or a quiet moment of reflection, self-care is about prioritizing yourself—not as an act of selfishness but as a foundation for supporting others.

The cornerstone of maintaining a healthy mind is **self-care**. Much like a car needs fuel and maintenance, our minds require regular attention to ensure they function optimally. Unfortunately, in the hustle of life, we often forget to take time for ourselves.

Self-care is not about being selfish—it's about prioritizing your mental health so that you can better support others. In this chapter, we explore ways to integrate mindfulness and self-compassion into your daily life through simple activities and practices.

From creating daily gratitude habits to journaling your feelings and exploring relaxation techniques, these practices are designed to nurture your mental well-being, helping you thrive in an often chaotic world.

The *Mind Aid Pitara* is filled with practical, easy-to-implement techniques to address everyday emotional struggles like guilt, jealousy, failure, and self-doubt. Think of it as a treasure chest of tools to heal your mind and nurture your inner strength.

Band-Aid Activities for Everyday Mind Blocks

Through the *Band-Aid Activities* in *Mind Aid Pitara*, you'll learn how to address common mental blocks with compassion and creativity. From simple exercises to shift negative thoughts to strategies for boosting self-esteem, these tips are designed to help you rebuild emotional resilience and embrace a happier, healthier version of yourself.

Final Thought

In a world where the hustle never stops, it is easy to forget that our minds need care, just like our bodies. The *Mind-Aid Pitara* is an invitation to embrace self-care and mental health awareness as part of your daily routine. By applying the techniques in this chapter, you will begin the journey of healing, growth, and resilience.

As I shared in *Decoding Mithya*, breaking through societal myths and misconceptions is key to achieving true freedom. When we stop judging ourselves and start embracing our mental health, we free ourselves to live with more peace, clarity, and joy.

As the author of *Decoding Mithya*, I urged readers to challenge societal myths. With *Mind Aid Pitara*, I invite you to challenge the myths within your own mind. Let's start this journey together, peeling back the layers of stigma and discovering the joy of living with clarity, purpose, and emotional well-being.

So, peel off the stigma, open the Pitara, and let the healing begin!

Chapter 2

Band-Aid Activity — A Brief Overview

Just as you would use a bandage or ointment for a minor physical wound, this "Band-Aid" activity offers quick, practical relief for everyday mental and emotional strains. It's a gentle first response—to hold you over until your natural resilience or additional support steps in. Think of it as **first aid** for the mind, giving you immediate tools to handle stress, anxiety, or self-doubt before these issues deepen.

Disclaimer

- The exercises shared here are meant for **mild emotional challenges**—much like treating a small cut or scrape.

- If you are experiencing severe distress, suicidal thoughts, or any urgent mental health concern, please seek professional help immediately.

- These methods do **not** replace therapy, counseling, or medical intervention.

By using these Band-Aid activities, you are taking a proactive step toward self-care, but remember: just as you'd see a doctor for a significant physical injury, it's equally important to seek professional mental health support when needed.

Activity 1: Mirror Work

Look in the Mirror, Meet Your Reflection

Disclaimer

This exercise is designed for mild emotional challenges—similar to tending to a small scrape with a bandage. If you are experiencing severe distress, suicidal thoughts, or any urgent mental health concern, please seek **immediate** professional help. This practice should complement, not replace, professional medical or psychological support.

What Is Mirror Work?

Mirror Work is a self-empowerment exercise where you literally face yourself—eye to eye—in a mirror. By speaking affirmations out loud while maintaining that connection, you send a powerful message of self-acceptance and compassion to your inner self. Much like peeling away the layers of societal myths in *Decoding Mithya*, Mirror Work helps uncover and heal the self-judgments that keep you from feeling confident and whole.

Key Principles of Mirror Work:

1. **Eye Contact**: Gaze into your own eyes to establish an authentic connection.

2. **Self-Acceptance**: Speak affirmations that reaffirm your worth and capability.

3. **Consistency**: Daily repetition creates new neural pathways for healthier self-talk.

What Issues Can Mirror Work Activity Address?

Mirror Work is a powerful technique that helps you confront and transform limiting beliefs. It can be especially helpful if you're dealing with:

- **Low Self-Esteem**: Feelings of inadequacy or constant self-criticism

- **Low Resilience**: Difficulty bouncing back from setbacks or stress

- **Low Confidence**: Fear of speaking up or taking risks

- **Stage Fright**: Anxiety about performing or being in the spotlight

- **Body Image Concerns**: Struggles with accepting your physical appearance

- **Social Anxiety**: Discomfort and nervousness around people or unfamiliar environments

Thought-Provoking Questions

Use these questions to deepen your self-reflection and help you apply Mirror Work when you most need it.

1. **What do I notice about my initial reaction to looking at myself in the mirror?**

   - Do I cringe, smile, or feel neutral?

   - What does this say about my current self-image?

2. **How do my body and mind react to positive affirmations?**

   - Do I feel resistance or comfort?

   - Which affirmation resonates the most?

3. **What patterns or limiting beliefs come up during the practice?**

   - Can I identify where these beliefs originated?

   - How might they be influencing my daily choices?

4. **When I feel anxious or upset during the day, could a quick mirror check-in help?**

   - What would I say to myself in those moments?

5. **How has my self-perception changed (if at all) after a week or more of daily mirror work?**

   - Do I notice any improvements in confidence or mood?

Using It in Moments of Need

- **Quick Pick-Me-Up**: If you're feeling overwhelmed by negative self-talk at work or school, take a brief bathroom break. Look at your reflection, repeat a calming affirmation, and breathe.

- **Before a Big Event**: Whether it's a presentation, a job interview, or a difficult conversation, a short mirror work session can help ground you and reduce nerves.

- **After Receiving Criticism**: Mirror Work can help you reframe criticism constructively rather than internalizing it as self-doubt.

Benefits Recap

- **Boosts Self-Esteem**: Regular mirror work helps replace harsh inner dialogue with supportive, nurturing words.

- **Fosters Emotional Resilience**: Affirmations help reorient negative thinking patterns toward growth and possibility.

- **Encourages Self-Compassion**: Meeting your own gaze with kindness shifts how you perceive your strengths and flaws.

- **Reinforces Positive Habits**: Daily repetition rewires the brain to favor self-belief over self-criticism.

Case Study: Neha's Journey from Stage Fear to Self-Assurance

Neha was a 16-year-old student who dreamed of being a singer. Despite her passion, she found herself paralyzed by stage fright. When asked to perform, her mind raced with doubts: "What if I forget the lyrics? What if people laugh?"

Desperate to overcome her anxiety, Neha tried Mirror Work. Here's how she did it:

1. **Preparation**: She chose a quiet spot in her room where she could be alone.

2. **Affirmations**: Neha wrote down five empowering statements such as:

   - "I am a confident performer."

   - "My voice deserves to be heard."

   - "I believe in my talent."

3. **Daily Practice**: Every morning and evening, she spent a few minutes looking into her eyes in a handheld mirror, repeating her affirmations out loud.

4. **Emotional Release**: Initially, Neha giggled at herself, feeling awkward. But as the days passed, she noticed her laughs turned into smiles of genuine self-encouragement.

5. **Progress**: Within three weeks, Neha mustered the courage to join her school's singing competition. Though nervous, she no longer felt paralyzed by self-doubt.

Over time, Neha's daily Mirror Work didn't just ease her stage fright—it instilled in her a new sense of self-worth.

How to Use Mirror Work

1. **Find Your Space**

   - Pick a calm environment where you can speak without interruptions.

   - Keep a small handheld mirror or stand in front of a larger mirror at eye level.

2. **Establish Eye Contact**

   - Take a few deep breaths.

   - Look into your eyes in the mirror, just as you would look into a friend's.

3. **Choose Your Affirmations**

   - Write down 3–5 statements that uplift and empower you.

- For example:

  - "I am worthy of success,"

  - "I trust myself,"

  - "I am becoming stronger every day."

4. **Speak Them Out Loud**

- Say each affirmation slowly and clearly.

- Notice any emotions that surface—whether it's laughter, tears, or discomfort—acknowledge them without judgment.

5. **Repeat Daily for 21 Days**

- Consistency is crucial. Treat this like a personal commitment.

- If you miss a day, simply resume the next. Over time, it will become a habit.

6. **Reflect and Record**

- After each session, jot down any noticeable changes in your self-talk or mood.

- At the end of each week, review your notes to see how far you've come.

Benefits of Mirror Work

- **Enhanced Self-Esteem**: By consistently affirming your worth, you gradually diminish negative self-perceptions.

- **Improved Resilience**: You learn to bounce back faster when life throws challenges your way.

- **Greater Confidence**: Speaking kindly to yourself can boost your ability to tackle public speaking, job interviews, or creative projects.

- **Sense of Inner Peace**: Daily self-affirmation quiets the internal critic, reducing stress and anxiety.

A Positive Note to End On

Much like discovering truths hidden beneath societal myths in *Decoding Mithya*, Mirror Work encourages you to look beneath the surface—beyond the fears, doubts, and judgments. By meeting your own gaze with kindness, you begin to rewrite the narrative that you are "not enough." Embracing the practice daily, even if only for a few moments, can spark a remarkable shift in how you perceive yourself and the world.

You are worthy. You are capable.
And most importantly, you are enough.

Worksheet for Practice

Use this worksheet to guide your daily mirror work. Feel free to adapt it according to your comfort and schedule.

1. **Choose Your Time & Space**

   - **Morning or Evening**: Select a time when you can spend a few minutes without distractions—right after you wake up or before bedtime often works best.

- **Calm Setting**: Find a quiet space with a mirror at eye level or use a handheld mirror.

2. **Set Your Intention**

- Ask yourself, "What do I hope to gain from this practice?"

- Possible answers could be: building self-esteem, reducing stress, finding inner peace, etc.

3. **Create or Select Your Affirmations**

- Write down 3–5 positive statements. Example:

  o "I am worthy of love and respect."

  o "I trust myself to handle life's challenges."

  o "I am growing and learning each day."

- Keep these affirmations nearby (on sticky notes, in a journal, or on your phone).

4. **Face the Mirror**

- Stand or sit comfortably, ensuring you can look straight into your own eyes.

- Take 3 deep breaths to center yourself.

5. **Maintain Eye Contact**

- Gaze into your reflection. If you feel awkward or silly, acknowledge these feelings without judgment. Remember, it's normal to feel self-conscious at first.

6. **Speak Your Affirmations Out Loud**

   - Say each affirmation clearly, pausing between each to let the words resonate.

   - Notice any physical or emotional reactions—tightness in the chest, flutter in the stomach, or even a smile.

7. **Observe Your Feelings**

   - After saying your affirmations, ask yourself: "How did that make me feel?"

   - If negative thoughts arise—"This is silly," "I don't believe this"—simply note them. Over time, consistent practice can help shift these limiting beliefs.

8. **Record Your Observations (Optional)**

   - Jot down any thoughts or feelings in a journal. Tracking your progress can help you see subtle changes over days or weeks.

9. **Repeat Daily for 21 Days**

   - Consistency is key. Much like forming any healthy habit, daily repetition will reinforce new patterns of self-talk.

Activity 2: The Power of Pause

Disclaimer

- This exercise is designed for **mild emotional challenges**—similar to tending to a small cut or scrape.

- If you are experiencing severe distress, suicidal thoughts, or any urgent mental health concern, please seek **professional help immediately**.

- These methods are intended to **complement**, not replace, therapy, counseling, or medical intervention.

> **"Memory is the residue of thought."**
> –Daniel Willingham

In *Decoding Mithya*, I spoke about unlearning societal myths that hold us back. In a similar vein, many of us need to unlearn the habit of reacting immediately to life's challenges without pausing to understand our own emotions. The **Power of Pause** is a simple yet profound practice that offers a chance to reflect, regroup, and respond—rather than react—to stressful situations.

Understanding the Power of Pause

The Power of Pause is about intentionally inserting a moment of stillness between **feeling** something and **reacting** to it. Instead of allowing our emotions (like anger or anxiety) to take the driver's seat, we consciously choose to **pause**. This brief interlude invites self-awareness, allowing us to make thoughtful choices rather than impulsive ones.

Which Situations and Issues Can It Help With?

- **Anger Management**: Giving yourself a moment to step back can prevent explosive outbursts.

- **Overthinking**: A pause disrupts the spiral of repetitive thoughts.

- **Negative Self-Talk**: Stopping to recognize critical inner dialogue can help you replace it with kinder, more realistic statements.

- **Stress and Anxiety**: Slowing down, even for a few seconds, calms the nervous system and provides mental clarity.

- **Low Mental Energy**: Constantly rushing drains our emotional reserves; pausing helps us recharge.

Aryan, a 25-year-old software developer, found himself constantly overthinking. He worried about missing deadlines and disappointing his team. Each day, he woke up feeling anxious and exhausted from mental chatter.

How Aryan Used the Power of Pause

1. **Conscious Decision to Pause**

   - Aryan set alarms on his phone to remind himself to stop working for a minute—just to breathe.

2. **P.A.U.S.E. Technique**

   - Whenever he noticed himself spiraling—*What if I can't finish this project on time?*—he would literally pause, take a deep breath, and run through each step:

- o **P**: Pause

- o **A**: And Breathe

- o **U**: Understand

- o **S**: Stop Blaming

- o **E**: Engage

3. **Rewriting the Narrative**

- He reminded himself that anxiety is the brain's natural response to perceived danger. Blaming himself for feeling anxious only magnified his stress.

4. **Positive Engagement**

- Instead of stewing in negativity, Aryan chose to tackle small, manageable tasks and celebrate each completed milestone.

Over a few weeks, Aryan noticed a reduction in his stress levels, and his work performance even improved. By integrating short pauses and mindful breathing into his day, Aryan broke the cycle of overthinking and restored balance to his routine.

Instructions: The P.A.U.S.E. Technique

1. **P – Pause**

- Stop whatever you're doing the moment you become aware of overthinking or anxiety.

- Allow yourself a brief mental and physical halt—no scrolling on your phone or jumping to another task.

2. **A – And Breathe**

   - Inhale deeply and exhale slowly, focusing on the rhythm of your breath.

   - Continue for several counts until you feel yourself settle into the present moment.

3. **U – Understand**

   - Recognize that worrying is the brain's protective mechanism—an attempt to keep you safe.

   - Acknowledge this response without judging yourself.

4. **S – Stop Blaming**

   - Release the urge to criticize or shame yourself for feeling anxious or stressed.

   - Replace self-blame with self-compassion: *I'm doing my best.*

5. **E – Engage**

   - Channel your energy into positive, solution-oriented actions.

   - Accept what you can't control and focus on what you *can* do.

Additional Tips

1. **Me Time**

   - Schedule daily check-ins with yourself.

   - Ask: *How am I feeling? Do I need more rest, social time, or a new skill challenge?*

2. **Power of Rising Strong**

- List the negative thoughts that hold you back.

- Remind yourself: *I can say NO to these negative beliefs.*

- Accept your life story—flaws and all—and allow yourself to emerge stronger.

Benefits

- **Self-Care**: Gives your mind a break, lowering stress levels.

- **Reduced Tension**: Encourages emotional regulation instead of knee-jerk reactions.

- **More Space, Less Anxiety**: Creates a mental buffer zone to assess your options.

- **Greater Happiness & Relaxation**: Helps you savor moments rather than rushing through them.

- **Increased Energy**: Frees up mental bandwidth, leaving you more refreshed.

Conclusion

Much like unmasking societal myths in *Decoding Mithya*, unlearning the habit of constant reactivity begins with simple shifts. The **Power of Pause** invites you to reclaim control over your emotional landscape. With each purposeful pause, you cultivate greater awareness, reduce stress, and build resilience—one breath at a time.

Worksheet for Practice

Use this worksheet to integrate **The Power of Pause** into your daily routine. Adapt it to your comfort and schedule, and remember, consistency is key.

1. **Identify Your Triggers**

   - Reflect on common situations where you tend to overreact or overthink (e.g., work emails, family conversations, public speaking).

   - Note these down so you can be vigilant about pausing when they occur.

2. **Set Reminders**

   - Use alarms or calendar notifications to cue yourself to pause and breathe.

   - Consistent reminders help turn pausing into a habit rather than a one-time effort.

3. **Practice P.A.U.S.E.**

   - **P**: Pause — Physically stop what you're doing.

   - **A**: And Breathe — Inhale deeply, exhale slowly.

   - **U**: Understand — Acknowledge your worries without self-judgment.

   - **S**: Stop Blaming — Shift from self-criticism to self-compassion.

   - **E**: Engage — Take a constructive action or accept what you can't change.

4. **Journal or Reflect Daily**

   - Spend a few minutes at the end of the day noting when you successfully paused and how it affected your mood.

   - If you missed an opportunity to pause, consider how you can catch it next time.

5. **Review Weekly**

   - Look over your notes to spot improvements.

   - Celebrate small wins, such as reduced anger or fewer overthinking episodes.

6. **Adapt as Needed**

   - Feel free to customize the technique. Maybe you need **longer** pauses or **additional** deep breaths before you feel grounded.

Activity 3: Emotional Freedom Technique (EFT)

Disclaimer

- This exercise is designed for **mild emotional challenges**—similar to tending to a small cut or scrape.

- If you are experiencing severe distress, suicidal thoughts, or any urgent mental health concern, please seek **professional help immediately**.

- These methods are intended to **complement**, not replace, therapy, counseling, or medical intervention.

EFT – Emotional Freedom Technique

Emotional Freedom Technique (EFT), often referred to as "tapping," combines elements of cognitive therapy and exposure therapy with light tapping on specific acupuncture points. It's based on the principle that tapping these points can help balance energy and reduce physical and emotional pain.

Life Challenges

EFT can be especially helpful if you're experiencing:

- **Pain Relief**

- **Weight Loss**

- **Stress**

- **Anxiety**

- **Feeling Low**

- **Fear**

EFT Technique: How It Works

1. **Sit Comfortably**

   - Find a quiet space.

   - Take a deep breath in, then exhale—repeat this for a total of **three times**.

2. **Begin Tapping (Karate Chop Point)**

   - Use your fingertips to gently tap on the *karate chop* part of your hand (the fleshy part beneath the pinkie/little finger).

   - Notice how you're feeling (anxious, stressed, nervous). Continue tapping throughout the following steps.

Method 1

1. **Identify the Issue**

   - Name the issue that is bothering you as you continue tapping (e.g., anxiety, pain, fear).

   - This is your primary focus for the activity.

2. **Rate the Intensity**

   - On a scale from **1–10** (with 10 being the most intense), rate how strongly you feel this issue.

   - Keep tapping as you assess your emotions.

3. "Tap In" and Repeat

- Think of a positive phrase (refer to the "EFT Script" below).

- Repeat it **7 times in your mind** as you continue tapping.

- Notice any shifts in how you feel.

Method 2

1. Repeat Steps 1–3 (Method 1)

- Identify the issue.

- Rate the intensity.

- Repeat your positive phrase.

2. Tap Through the Sequence Points

- Now tap each of the **8 EFT points** in sequence:

  1. **Eyebrow Point**: Inner points of your eyebrows, just above the bridge of your nose.

  2. **Side of Eye**: The bone along the outside corner of your eyes.

  3. **Under Eye**: The bone directly under your eyes.

  4. **Under Nose**: Between your nose and upper lip.

  5. **Chin Point**: The crease below your bottom lip and above your chin.

  6. **Collarbone Point**: About one inch below and one inch to the side of where your collarbones meet.

7. **Under Arm**: On your ribcage, about four inches below your armpit.

8. **Top of Head**: The crown of your head.

- **Continue tapping** each point consecutively, repeating the **EFT Script (positive phrase) 3 times** at each point.

Tapping – EFT Script

Repeat **3 times** at each point:

"Even though I am having this anxiety/pain/fear,

I accept myself / I will love and integrate that part of me,

and I am feeling relaxed/good/confident."

5. Rate the Intensity Again

- After one full sequence, check in with yourself: *"How do I feel now on a scale of 1–10?"*

- If the intensity is still high, **repeat Steps 3–4** until your feelings are reduced to around **2–3** on the scale.

Note

It's normal if you don't feel a significant change in your emotional state after just one round of tapping. Continue with Steps 1–5 until the intensity of your feelings or issue decreases.

Benefits

- **Simple and Painless**: Easy to learn and apply almost anywhere.

- **Self-Guided**: No therapist required, making it more accessible and less expensive.

- **Less Time-Consuming**: Quick results with consistent practice.

- **Specific Emotional Focus**: You can tailor EFT to address your unique life challenges.

- **Power to Heal**: Empowers you to manage your emotional well-being.

- **Less Distress**: Helps lower the stress that contributes to various issues.

- **Natural, No Side-Effects**: A holistic approach without medication.

Worksheet for Practice

Use this worksheet to guide your daily tapping practice. Adapt it as needed to fit your personal schedule and comfort level.

1. **Identify the Issue**

   - What are you feeling today? Anxiety? Pain? Fear?

   - Write it down or say it aloud.

2. **Rate Your Intensity**

   - On a scale of 1–10, note your initial level of distress.

   - Example: "I feel my anxiety is at a 7."

3. **Choose Your EFT Script**

   - Use the basic script or create your own personalized version:

"Even though I'm experiencing (issue), I accept and love myself, and I am feeling (positive state)."

4. **Tap the Karate Chop Point**

   - Begin tapping while repeating your script in your mind or out loud.

   - Continue for several taps.

5. **Move Through the 8 Points**

   - Tap each point (eyebrow, side of eye, etc.) **3 times** with your script.

   - Notice any shifts in mood or body sensations as you tap.

6. **Reassess**

   - Rate your level of intensity again (1–10).

   - If still high, repeat the sequence until it decreases to a comfortable level.

7. **Reflect and Record** (Optional)

   - Jot down any changes or insights in a journal.

   - Note improvements over days or weeks of consistent practice.

A Positive Note to End On

EFT is much like the process of unlearning myths in *Decoding Mithya*: each tap helps you release old stories and emotional blocks, paving the way for clarity and renewed self-confidence. Over time, you'll discover that this simple, self-guided technique can create significant shifts in how you handle stress, anxiety, and everyday challenges.

Activity 4: Energy Management & Energy Detox

Disclaimer

- This exercise is designed for **mild lifestyle and productivity challenges**—similar to tending to a small cut or scrape.

- If you are experiencing severe distress, burnout, or any urgent mental health concern, please seek **professional help immediately**.

- These methods are intended to **complement**, not replace, therapy, counseling, or medical intervention.

Introduction: Why Manage Your Energy?

It's easy to calculate how long you work each day, but can you calculate how much **energy** you expend daily? While the number of hours in a day is fixed, your **quantity and quality of energy** can vary greatly. By learning to manage your energy more effectively, you can boost productivity and overall well-being.

Life Challenges

This activity is especially helpful if you're dealing with:

- **Procrastination**

- **Time Management**

- **Decision Fatigue**

- **Decision Making**

- **Losing Focus & Interest**

Part I: Manage Your Energy

1. Energy Awareness

Our energy levels naturally fluctuate throughout the day (in ~90-minute cycles called **ultradian rhythms**). Several factors influence these highs and lows:

- **Sleep**

- **Food**

- **Me Time**

- **Social Circles** (Who do you spend time with?)

- **Thoughts/Emotions/Purpose**

Key Tip: Be aware of your "**Peak Energy Period**" and schedule your most important or demanding tasks during that time.

2. The "WHY" in Our Life

Without a clear purpose or motivation, you risk wasting both time and energy. Purpose fuels personal energy—when you know **why** you're doing something, your **inner drive** increases.

Action Step:

- Spend 5–10 minutes journaling or reflecting on your "**why**" for any major goal or task.

- Notice how clarifying your purpose ignites motivation and sustains momentum.

3. Develop Habits – Save Energy

Habits are the **foundation** of lifestyle design. While forming a new habit can initially require more focus and energy, once it's established, it runs on autopilot—saving both time and energy.

- **Example**: Roughly 40% of our daily actions are habitual. You don't need to think through these actions each time, thus conserving mental energy.

- **Tip**: A **to-do list** can feel tiring because each item demands a new decision. Turning frequent tasks into habits reduces decision-making strain.

4. Avoid Decision Fatigue

Each decision you make consumes **mental energy**. The more decisions you face in a day, the more **decision fatigue** builds up, draining your willpower and focus.

- **Trick**: Reduce the number of decisions through **elimination, automation,** or **delegation**.

- **Example**: Choose your outfit the night before to avoid an extra morning decision.

5. Stop Multitasking—Start Monotasking

Multitasking often leads to errors and mental strain, causing you to spend even **more** time fixing mistakes. **Monotasking**, or focusing on one task at a time, lessens the cognitive load and **conserves energy**.

Reminder: Switching between tasks can deplete your energy due to the mental "start-up cost" each time you switch focus.

Part II: Energy Detox

"Stop giving away your energy to people, things, emotions that aren't serving you!"

8 Ways to Take Your 'Energy Back'

1. **Don't Waste Energy Complaining**

   - Shift from complaining to **finding solutions**.

   - Example: *"Better to light a candle than curse the darkness."*

2. **Accept Responsibility for How You Feel**

   - Statements like *"People don't understand me"* hand control of your emotions to others.

   - Embrace your emotions—whether positive or negative—without blaming external factors.

3. **Establish Healthy Boundaries**

   - Guilt and fear of confrontation can drain your energy.

   - Speak up for yourself and set clear emotional limits.

4. **Practice Forgiveness**

   - Holding onto grudges saps your mental and emotional energy.

   - Forgiving doesn't condone the wrong; it frees **you** from carrying anger.

5. **Know Your Values**

   - Without clear personal values, you become a **passenger** in life instead of the **driver**.

   - Clarify

   - what matters most to you, and let those values guide decisions.

6. **Avoid Unproductive Thoughts**

   - Control the mental loops of negativity.

   - Example: Complaining about your 8-hour workday for 12–15 hours means you're **giving** it even more of your time.

7. **Avoid Victim Mentality**

   - Phrases like *"I have to do everything!"* imply helplessness.

   - Own your choices and actions; remember, you **always** have options.

8. **Increase Your Self-Worth and Stand Out**

   - Don't be a "people-pleaser" at the expense of your own goals or well-being.

   - Accept feedback, but don't let anyone's opinion define your **self-worth**.

Worksheet for Practice

Use this worksheet to help you **manage your energy** more effectively and **detox** from draining habits.

1. **Map Your Energy Cycles**

   - **Morning, Afternoon, Evening**: Track your energy for a week to identify peak periods.

   - Schedule high-impact tasks during your peak hours.

2. **Clarify Your "Why"**

   - Write down one key goal.

   - Below it, list **3 reasons** why you want to achieve it.

   - Reflect on how these reasons energize you.

3. **Create One New Habit**

   - Choose a routine task you can automate (e.g., setting out clothes, meal prep).

   - Practice it daily for at least **3 weeks** to embed it as a habit.

4. **Eliminate or Delegate**

   - Look at your to-do list.

   - Identify **1–2 tasks** you can either **eliminate** or **delegate** to someone else.

5. **Monotasking Challenge**

   - Pick a significant task. Work on it for **25 minutes** without switching to anything else.

   - Notice how your focus and energy hold up.

6. **Energy Detox Checklist**

- **Complaints**: Catch yourself complaining. Replace it with a solution-focused statement.

- **Boundaries**: Say "no" at least once this week to protect your energy.

- **Self-Worth**: Write down **3 affirmations** that reflect your values and strengths.

A Positive Note to End On

Much like uncovering societal myths in *Decoding Mithya*, **unlearning** the habits that drain your energy requires self-awareness and a willingness to change. By actively managing your energy and cutting out what doesn't serve you, you take control—leading to greater **productivity**, **focus**, and overall **fulfillment**.

Activity 5: Reclaiming the Childlike Joy

Disclaimer

- This exercise is designed for **mild emotional challenges**—similar to tending to a small cut or scrape.

- If you are experiencing severe distress, suicidal thoughts, or any urgent mental health concern, please seek **professional help immediately**.

- These methods are intended to **complement**, not replace, therapy, counseling, or medical intervention.

Introduction: "Be Happy for No Reason"

"Be happy for no reason, like a child. If you are happy for a reason, you're in trouble, because that reason can be taken from you."

Many of us fondly recall childhood as a carefree time—no major responsibilities, fewer worries, and an abundance of curiosity. Yet, as we grow older, we often lose touch with that **unconditional joy**. This activity explores ways to **reclaim** that childlike happiness, even amidst adult responsibilities.

Life Challenges

This activity is especially helpful if you're dealing with:

- **Sharmaji Kya Kahenge Syndrome** (Social Stigma)

- **Need for Social Approval**

- **Anxiety**

- **Pessimism**

- **Jealousy**

Tips & Techniques: Reclaiming Childlike Joy

1. Stop Caring About What Others Think

As we age, we often become overly concerned with **how others perceive us**. Children, however, move through the world with fewer inhibitions.

- **Action Step**: Identify one behavior you've been holding back due to fear of judgment. Challenge yourself to do it anyway—like wearing a bold outfit or voicing your opinion in a meeting.

2. Embrace Curiosity

Research shows that **curiosity** correlates with increased happiness and reduced anxiety. Children ask endless questions, driven by pure wonder.

- **Practical Tip**: Make it a habit to ask "*Why?*" or "*How?*" in your daily life. Whether it's learning a new recipe or exploring a hobby, curiosity can reignite your sense of **wonder**.

3. Be Honest and Clear

Children are often straightforward; adults tend to sugarcoat or avoid tough conversations.

- **Key Insight**: **Stop** making excuses or deflecting with humor when something bothers you. Instead, practice genuine, direct communication.

- **Outcome**: Honesty fosters **authentic relationships** and reduces pent-up frustration.

4. Don't Be Afraid to Show Emotions

From tears to laughter, children aren't ashamed of their emotional expressions. Studies indicate that **crying** can lower blood pressure and reduce stress hormones.

- **Reminder**: Holding back tears often prolongs distress. Give yourself permission to **feel**. Release can be **healing**.

5. Stop Holding Grudges

Children quarrel one moment and play together the next—they rarely hold onto bitterness.

- **Action Step**: Reflect on someone or something you've been **resentful** toward. Ask yourself, *"How does holding this grudge serve me?"* If the answer is it **doesn't**, choose forgiveness for your own peace of mind.

A Childlike Perspective on Optimism

"See good life events as self-made and bad life events as transient. Remember, nothing is permanent in life."

- **Core Idea**: Children bounce back quickly because they view negative experiences as temporary. Adopting this mindset can **cultivate resilience**.

Worksheet for Practice

Use this worksheet to guide your journey back to a **childlike sense of joy**.

1. **Identify 3 "Childlike" Qualities**

   - Examples: **Playfulness, Curiosity, Honesty**.

   - Write them down and brainstorm ways to integrate them into your daily routine.

2. **Action Against "Sharmaji Kya Kahenge Syndrome"**

   - List **1–2** behaviors or expressions you've been avoiding due to fear of social judgment.

   - Commit to challenging at least **one** of these beliefs this week.

3. **Practice Emotional Honesty**

   - Each day, note a moment you felt like **withholding** your true feelings.

   - Ask yourself, "What's the honest, childlike approach here?" and follow through in a kind but direct manner.

4. **Curiosity Challenge**

   - Pick an unfamiliar topic (e.g., a foreign cuisine or a historical event).

   - Spend **15 minutes** learning about it, purely for fun—no pressure or goal, just **exploration**.

5. **Letting Go of a Grudge**

   - Write down a situation or person you hold resentment toward.

   - In a journal, explore **why** you're holding onto it and what it might take to forgive or let go.

6. **Embrace Optimism**

- Note one **negative** event this week.

- Reframe it as a temporary setback and find **one** small lesson or silver lining.

A Positive Note to End On

True maturity isn't just about handling responsibilities; it's also about retaining **childlike wonder** and **unconditional joy**. As you peel away layers of social stigma and self-imposed expectations—much like revealing truths in *Decoding Mithya*—you'll rediscover that **simple, carefree happiness** can be a choice you cultivate every day.

Activity 6: Taming the Monkey Mind

Disclaimer

- This exercise is designed for **mild emotional challenges**—similar to tending to a small cut or scrape.

- If you are experiencing severe distress, suicidal thoughts, or any urgent mental health concern, please seek **professional help immediately**.

- These methods are intended to **complement**, not replace, therapy, counseling, or medical intervention.

Life Challenges

This activity is especially helpful if you're dealing with:

- **Fixed Mindset**

- **Negative Self-Talk**

- **Overthinking**

- **Low Self-Esteem**

The 3 Wise Monkeys and the "Monkey Mind"

Mahatma Gandhi and his Three Wise Monkeys have long been symbols urging us to avoid evil in what we **see**, what we **hear**, and what we **speak**. Though their origins may date back to Confucius, Taoism, and Japanese Shintoism, the core message has stood the test of time:

"Do not see evil. Do not hear evil. Do not speak evil."

But why monkeys?

Gautam Buddha introduced the concept of the **Monkey Mind**—the restless nature of our thoughts, leaping from one concern to the next. In this light, the Three Wise Monkeys represent a caution against letting your mind run wild with **negative** or **harmful** thinking.

In modern terms:

- **Do not SEE or IMAGINE evil things** (in your mind).

- **Do not LISTEN to negative self-talk** (in your mind).

- **Do not SPEAK negativity about yourself** (in your mind), or in simpler words, **think before you speak.**

Technique: BANANA for Taming the Monkey Mind

B – Be Engaged

- Engage your mind in an activity that **fully absorbs** your attention (e.g., painting, solving puzzles, exercising).

- When your focus is on the task at hand, there's less "brain space" left for the monkey mind to chatter.

A – A Journaling Practice

- Set aside a **regular journaling time** each day to address your mind's worries.

- Writing helps you **process** thoughts rather than letting them swirl endlessly.

N – Notice 5 Things

- Play the **Game of Fives**: Pause your thoughts and notice **five things** in your environment—things you can **see, hear,** or **smell.**

- This quick **grounding technique** brings you back to the present moment.

A – Activity to Calm Your Mind

- **Mindfulness**—whether through meditation, deep breathing, or focused attention—naturally quiets a busy mind.

- Integrating small mindfulness breaks throughout the day (even 1–2 minutes at a time) can yield significant benefits.

N – Negative Self-Talk Habit

- **Identify** your patterns of negative self-talk.

- **Reframe** them:

  1. **Acknowledge** negative thoughts without self-criticism.

  2. **Validate** them with self-compassion (it's normal to have such thoughts sometimes).

  3. **Externalize** by writing them down.

  4. **Flexibly generate** more realistic, alternative thoughts.

A – Acknowledge

- Instead of **criticizing** yourself for negative thoughts, simply **acknowledge** them.

- You can't always control if they pop up, but you **can** decide how to respond.

Worksheet for Practice

1. **Identify Your Monkey Mind Triggers**

   - Write down three situations or times of day when your thoughts start jumping uncontrollably (e.g., late at night, before a presentation, during commutes).

2. **Apply the BANANA Technique**

   B: Be Engaged

   - Pick **one** absorbing activity (e.g., coloring, reading, light exercise) to redirect your attention daily.

   A: A Journaling Practice

   - Start with just **5 minutes** of journaling in the morning or evening to dump your worries on paper.

   N: Notice 5 Things

   - Practice this grounding exercise whenever anxiety or negative thoughts spike.

   A: Activity to Calm Your Mind

   - Integrate a short **mindful break**: a few deep breaths, or a mini body-scan.

N: Negative Self-Talk Habit

- Keep track of negative phrases in a small notebook; consciously **reframe** them.

A: Acknowledge

- Each time negativity arises, say: "I notice this thought. It doesn't define me."

3. **Track Your Progress**

- Over the next week, rate how often you feel overwhelmed by your monkey mind (on a scale of 1–10).

- Note any improvement after applying BANANA for a few days.

4. **Reflect & Adapt**

- Which part of BANANA was most **effective** for you?

- How can you integrate it into your daily routine more seamlessly?

A Positive Note to End On

Much like peeling away layers of misconception in *Decoding Mithya*, taming the "monkey mind" involves **awareness**, **patience**, and **consistent practice**. By applying BANANA—engaging in mindful activities, journaling, grounding, and reframing negative self-talk—you'll find greater **clarity** and **calm** in your thoughts. Remember, the goal is not to stop thinking entirely but to **guide your mind** toward more constructive and compassionate pathways.

Activity 7: Mandala Art Journaling

Disclaimer

- This exercise is designed for **mild emotional challenges**—similar to tending to a small cut or scrape.

- If you are experiencing severe distress, severe anxiety or depression, suicidal thoughts, or any urgent mental health concern, please seek **professional help immediately**.

- These methods are intended to **complement**, not replace, therapy, counseling, or medical intervention.

Introduction: "Art Journaling as a Visual Conversation with Yourself"

Art journaling allows you to express your internal world—your emotions, thoughts, and energies—in a **tangible**, **visual** form. It can reduce stress, alleviate anxiety, improve sleep, and enhance concentration by channeling your mental chatter into creative output.

Life Challenges

This activity is especially helpful if you're dealing with:

- **Stress**

- **Anxiety**

- **Sleep Disorder**

- **Concentration Difficulties**

What is Mandala?

Mandala comes from the Sanskrit word meaning "magic circle" or simply "circle." The **circular designs** symbolize life's never-ending cycle and the interconnectedness of all things. According to psychologist **Carl Jung**, Mandalas represent one's **collective unconscious**—a gateway to deeper self-awareness.

Mandala Art Therapy

Creating art within a circle (Mandala) is a powerful therapeutic tool that can reveal hidden facets of our personality. By spontaneously drawing shapes, symbols, and images inside the Mandala, we bring forth our **subconscious thoughts**, feelings, and energies. The Mandala becomes a **mirror of the SELF**, offering insight into fears, desires, anxieties, and hopes that might otherwise remain hidden.

Creating the Circle of Life – Your Mandala

1. **Relax and Meditate**

   - Spend a few minutes **quieting your mind** through deep breathing or guided meditation.

2. **Visual Imagery**

   - Notice the **images** appearing in your mind. These might be shapes, symbols, or colors.

3. **Start Doodling**

   - Take any **medium** you like—markers, crayons, sketch pens— and begin **spontaneously** filling your Mandala circle with what comes to mind.

- Allow the art to **flow** without overthinking.

4. **Trust Your Subconscious**

   - Some shapes or patterns may come directly from the **images** you saw during meditation.

   - Others may **emerge** from your subconscious, revealing hidden aspects of your inner world.

5. **Holistic Representation**

   - Once finished, you have a **holistic** snapshot of your current **inner state**.

   - Think of it as a **mental fingerprint**, unique to you in this moment.

6. **Observe the Patterns**

   - The shapes, colors, and symbols represent **mental patterns** and **energies**. Try to **translate** or interpret these elements.

Translating Your Mandala

"Everything that shows up in your Mandala is a vehicle for your awakening."

Use these **questions** as a guide to explore what your Mandala might be communicating:

1. **Patterns & Themes**

   - Do you notice any **hot spots** or areas that stand out?

   - Are there sections that feel **neglected** or **ignored**?

2. **Current or Past Issues**

   - Does any part of the Mandala relate to a **current** or **past** problem?

3. **Attention Needed**

   - Is there a **part of yourself** within the Mandala that requires more care or acknowledgment?

4. **Negative Influences or Blocked Energies**

   - Do you see any **symbols** or **colors** that signify **tension**, **pain**, or **obstacles**?

5. **Pain, Trauma, Hope, or Dreams**

   - Can you identify any areas that seem to represent **hurt**, **healing**, or **aspirations**?

6. **Telling a Story**

   - Does your Mandala suggest a **narrative**? Are there characters, landscapes, or scenes that might relate to your life experiences?

7. **Seeing the Bigger Picture**

   - Step back and **look** at your Mandala as a whole.

   - What **feelings** or **messages** does it convey when you view it in its entirety?

Note: No book or website can give you a definitive translation. **You** are the ultimate interpreter of your Mandala. In some cases, a qualified

therapist or **specialist** can help guide you, but the core understanding lies within you.

Worksheet for Practice

Use this worksheet to deepen your Mandala Art Journaling experience.

1. **Preparation & Centering**

   - Write down how you feel **before** you begin (e.g., anxious, tired, hopeful).

   - Set a timer for **5–10 minutes** of quiet meditation or deep breathing.

2. **Mandala Creation**

   - Draw a large circle on a blank page.

   - Allow **free expression**—no rules or constraints.

3. **Immediate Impressions**

   - After you finish, note your **initial reaction**. What stands out first?

4. **Detailed Observation**

   - Spend a few minutes **scanning** your Mandala. Which shapes or colors catch your attention the most?

5. **Answer the Translation Questions**

   - Refer to the **questions** above to delve into your Mandala's possible meanings.

- Jot down your reflections in a **journal**.

6. **Post-Art Reflection**

   - Rate how you feel **after** creating your Mandala (on a scale of 1–10 for calmness, insight, relief, etc.).

   - Compare it to your **pre-art** state.

7. **Integration**

   - Consider if there's an **action** you can take based on your Mandala's insights. For instance, if you notice a "neglected" portion, it might reflect an area of life you need to nurture.

A Positive Note to End On

Mandala art therapy is a doorway to your **deepest self**—an introspective tool that reveals how your mind and soul intersect in creative ways. Much like the process of **self-discovery** in *Decoding Mithya*, every mark on your Mandala holds a piece of your **story**. By engaging with these visual insights, you may discover **fresh perspectives**, **untapped strengths**, and a profound sense of **inner balance**.

Activity 8: Transforming Limiting Beliefs

Disclaimer

- This exercise is designed for **mild emotional challenges**—similar to tending to a small cut or scrape.

- If you are experiencing severe distress, suicidal thoughts, or any urgent mental health concern, please seek **professional help immediately**.

- These methods are intended to **complement**, not replace, therapy, counseling, or medical intervention.

Introduction: "Don't Limit Your Challenges, Challenge Your Limits"

Limiting beliefs can create invisible walls that keep us from reaching our full potential. By learning how to **identify** and **reframe** these beliefs, we can transform them into a powerful force for **growth** and **self-discovery**.

Life Challenges

This activity is especially helpful if you're dealing with:

- **Low Self-Esteem**

- **Low Emotional Quotient**

- **Negative Self-Beliefs**

Understanding Beliefs

Our beliefs form the **lens** through which we see ourselves, others, and the world. They define what is **possible** or **impossible**, and heavily influence:

- **Emotions**

- **Actions**

- **Judgments** (right vs. wrong, safe vs. dangerous, worthy vs. unworthy)

When beliefs become **limiting**, they can hold us back from living confidently and purposefully. The goal is to **identify** and **shift** these beliefs from a negative frame to an **empowering** one.

Step 1: Awareness

"Areas of your life where you are not getting what you want … those are your limiting beliefs."

1. **Identify Your Limiting Beliefs**

   - **Write down** the areas of your life where you feel stuck or keep failing.

   - Consider what thoughts or beliefs might be **underlying** these struggles.

2. **Question Prompts**

   (a) What part of your life are you dissatisfied with or not seeing results?

(b) Which areas have you tried to improve but still feel stuck?

(c) Where do you feel **unhappy** or **discontented**?

(d) In which situations do you feel **weak, powerless,** or **incompetent**?

3. **Honest Answers**

- The truths you uncover (e.g., "I'm not good enough," "I can never succeed at X") reveal your **limiting beliefs**.

Step 2: Contemplating

"Get your focus back to your dreams, desires, and qualities."

1. **Revisit Your Wishes and Strengths**

- Write down **3–5** things you **truly** desire in life.

- List your **core qualities** or **strengths** (e.g., creativity, resilience, empathy).

2. **Identify Self-Sabotage**

- Notice any "I can't … because" or "I am … because" statements.

- These phrases indicate **internal roadblocks** that keep you tied to old beliefs.

3. **Refocus on Solutions**

- Instead of **lamenting** disappointments, ask: *"How can I move forward or do things differently?"*

- This shift in mindset opens the door to **possibility** rather than defeat.

Step 3: Reframe

"Turning negative beliefs into empowering beliefs takes practice and conscious effort."

1. **List Out Limiting Beliefs**

   Examples:

   - **Limiting**: "I am ugly and unappealing."

   - **Empowering**: "I am attractive and desirable."

   - **Limiting**: "Most people are dishonest and will cheat me."

   - **Empowering**: "Most people are honest and kind."

   - **Limiting**: "I'm a terrible public speaker."

   - **Empowering**: "I can excel at speaking if I research and practice."

2. **Create Positive Counter-Statements**

   - Replace "I can't" with "I can if I …"

   - Turn "I'm not capable" into "I am capable when I …"

3. **Write & Review**

   - Keep your new **empowering statements** visible (on your phone, a sticky note, or a journal).

   - Review them **daily** to reinforce the mindset shift.

Step 4: Action

"Your body and mind need time to rewire and fully accept new beliefs."

1. **Start Small**

   - Taking small, **safe risks** helps challenge old beliefs and proves them wrong.

   - Celebrate **small victories**—they reinforce that your new belief is working.

2. **Step Outside Your Comfort Zone**

   - Your subconscious may resist by making you feel "bad" or "wrong" for leaving old habits behind.

   - Consistent, **gradual** exposure to new experiences helps solidify empowering beliefs.

3. **Patience & Perseverance**

   - Old beliefs won't vanish overnight.

   - Consistent **practice**, **reflection**, and **reinforcement** are crucial.

Key Insight

"Our limiting beliefs can undo our current progress in life. By shifting your mindset and challenging what holds you back, you gain both self-confidence and self-awareness."

Worksheet for Practice

1. **Identify One Limiting Belief**

   - **Write it down** in a sentence (e.g., "I'm not good enough to start my own business.").

2. **Explore the Roots**

   - Ask yourself: *"When did I first start believing this?"* or *"Has someone in my past reinforced this?"*

3. **Reframe Statement**

   - Turn it into an **empowering** one (e.g., "I have the potential to start and grow my own business with the right plan and dedication.").

4. **Action Step**

   - Pick **one small action** that supports your new belief (e.g., research one aspect of starting a business, like budgeting or networking events).

5. **Track & Reflect**

   - After a week, revisit your journal.

   - **Note** any shifts in perspective or outcomes.

6. **Ongoing Practice**

   - **Repeat** Steps 1–5 for other limiting beliefs that arise.

   - Gradually, you'll build a toolkit of empowering beliefs and corresponding actions.

A Positive Note to End On

Transforming limiting beliefs is like changing the lens through which you view life—it can **clarify** your vision and **expand** your horizons. Much like the journey in *Decoding Mithya*, each step peels away societal or self-imposed myths that keep you from recognizing your **true potential**. By actively reframing and acting upon new beliefs, you'll cultivate the **confidence** and **purpose** needed to thrive.

Activity 9: Healthy Mind Platter

Disclaimer

- This exercise is designed for **mild emotional challenges**—similar to tending to a small cut or scrape.

- If you are experiencing severe distress, suicidal thoughts, or any urgent mental health concern, please seek **professional help immediately**.

- These methods are intended to **complement**, not replace, therapy, counseling, or medical intervention.

Introduction: "Health is Wealth"

The famous proverb **"Health is Wealth"** reminds us that both **physical** and **mental** well-being are the true measures of a life well-lived. No amount of monetary wealth can substitute for good health. Just as a balanced **food pyramid** sustains our physical body, a balanced **mental health platter** keeps our minds resilient, positive, and thriving.

Life Challenges

This activity is especially helpful if you're dealing with:

- **Low Focus**

- **Anxiety**

- **Stress**

- **Negative Overthinking**

Dr. Dan Siegel's Healthy Mind Platter

There's **no fixed recipe** for mental wellness—just as there is no single best combination of foods for everyone. The idea is to **choose** and **blend** the elements that work best for **you**. According to Dr. Dan Siegel, a **healthy mind platter** consists of **seven essential ingredients** for a balanced mental life:

1. Focussing Time

- **What It Is**: Time-block specific chunks of your day to concentrate on an important task.

- **Key Tip**: Schedule these tasks when your **energy** is at its peak, ensuring maximum productivity.

- **Example**: If you're most alert in the morning, block that time for creative or complex work.

2. Time for Play

- **Why It Matters**: Play triggers the release of **endorphins**, enhancing vitality and reducing stress.

- **Quote**: *"We don't stop playing because we grow old; we grow old because we stop playing."* —George Bernard Shaw

- **Example**: Engaging in a favorite hobby, playing a sport, or simply goofing around with friends or family.

3. Connecting Time

- **Purpose**: Strengthening bonds with loved ones and nature activates our brain's "relational circuitry."

- **Practical Tip**: Practice **mindful communication**—listen deeply, maintain eye contact, and respond with empathy.

- **Example:** Plan a nature walk with a friend or have a tech-free meal with family.

4. Physical Time

- **Health Benefit**: Movement isn't just good for your body—research shows it also **strengthens the brain**.

- **Reminder**: *"Sitting is the new smoking."*

- **Ideas**: Dancing, yoga, taking the stairs, playing with pets, or going for a brisk walk.

5. Time In

- **What It Is**: Turning inward for self-reflection, focusing on feelings and thoughts.

- **Method**: Integrate **mindfulness** or "ME time" to check in with your inner state.

- **Example**: A short, 5-minute meditation session or a journaling habit each evening.

6. Down Time

- **Goal**: Let your mind **wander** without a specific plan, schedule, or goal.

- **Why It Helps**: This mental "white space" allows your brain to **recharge**.

- **Example**: Enjoy a quiet moment with a favorite beverage, keeping gadgets off and responsibilities momentarily on hold.

7. Sleep Time

- **Importance**: Sleep allows the brain to **rest** and **recover** from daily stresses.

- **Tip**: Turn off electronic devices at least **60 minutes** before bedtime to help your mind wind down.

- **Outcome**: Quality sleep improves mood, focus, and overall mental health.

Worksheet for Practice

Use this worksheet to **personalize** Dr. Dan Siegel's Healthy Mind Platter for your own mental wellness routine.

1. **Assess Your Current Routine**

   - Write down how much time you currently devote to each "ingredient" (Focusing, Play, Connecting, Physical, Time In, Down Time, Sleep).

2. **Set a Small Goal for Each Platter Ingredient**

   - **Focusing Time**: ___ minutes of dedicated work/study.

   - **Play Time**: ___ minutes of unstructured fun.

   - **Connecting Time**: One specific way you'll deepen a relationship (e.g., a phone call, shared activity).

   - **Physical Time**: ___ minutes or steps (if tracking) per day.

- **Time In**: ___ minutes of mindfulness or journaling daily.

- **Down Time**: ___ minutes of guilt-free relaxation.

- **Sleep**: Target bedtime and wake-up time, and how you'll **disconnect** before bed.

3. **Reflect**

- After a week, evaluate how balanced your "Mind Platter" feels.

- Note any areas where you struggled or excelled.

4. **Adjust & Experiment**

- Remember, there's no **one-size-fits-all**. Tweak the durations and activities until you find the **best combination** for you.

5. **Identify Barriers**

- Are you consistently skipping certain elements (e.g., Down Time)?

- What might help you **overcome** these barriers (e.g., scheduling a reminder, enlisting support from family/friends)?

6. **Celebrate Small Wins**

- Recognize each day's **progress**, no matter how minor.

- Positive reinforcement encourages long-term habit changes.

A Positive Note to End On

Much like the balanced approach we discuss in *Decoding Mithya*, achieving a **healthy mind** involves blending various elements to create a life that supports **both** your body and psyche. By adopting Dr. Dan Siegel's seven essential "nutrients," you'll cultivate **resilience**, **clarity**, and a deeper sense of **fulfillment**. Remember, **health truly is wealth**, and your mind deserves the **richest** nourishment you can give it.

Activity 10: D-BELLS for Mind Strengthening

Disclaimer

- This exercise is designed for **mild emotional challenges**—similar to tending to a small cut or scrape.

- If you are experiencing severe distress, suicidal thoughts, or any urgent mental health concern, please seek **professional help immediately**.

- These methods are intended to **complement**, not replace, therapy, counseling, or medical intervention.

Introduction: "Dumbbells for Muscles, D-BELLS for the Mind"

Just as **dumbbells** can help build physical strength, **D-BELLS** is a simple yet powerful tool to **fortify** your mind. In a world filled with overthinking, multitasking, and endless demands, consciously practicing kindness, patience, and healthy boundaries can prevent mental overload and promote emotional resilience.

Life Challenges

This activity is especially helpful if you're dealing with:

- **Overthinking**

- **Multitasking**

- **Feeling Overburdened**

D-BELLS Technique

1. **D – Do (Be Kind)**

   - **Why It Helps**: Choosing kindness intentionally can stop automatic negative responses, improving your mood and relationships.

   - **Practical Example**: Send a thoughtful message to a friend, refrain from unkind words—even if you feel provoked.

2. **B – Be Patient**

   - **Key Insight**: *"Patience is bitter, but its fruit is sweet."*

   - **Implementation**: When facing delays or irritations, pause before reacting. Take a deep breath or count to five. Train yourself to respond calmly rather than impulsively.

3. **E – Escape (the Need to Sound Clever at Another's Expense)**

   - **What It Means**: Avoid caustic jokes or remarks aimed at boosting your ego by bringing someone else down.

   - **Action Step**: The next time you're tempted to make a sarcastic comment, check if it hurts someone. If so, refrain and redirect the conversation.

4. **L – Leave Early for Work**

   - **Benefit**: Disciplined time management reduces stress and mental clutter.

- **Method**: Try heading out 10–15 minutes earlier than usual. Enjoy the buffer time to organize your thoughts or review priorities.

5. **L – Leave Work at Work**

   - **Challenge**: Constant beeping, blinking devices bind us to work 24/7.

   - **Solution**: Create a ritual to "clock out"—turn off work notifications, change into comfy clothes, or take a quick walk. This signals your brain to **shift** into personal mode.

6. **S – Sort Out Differences Harmoniously**

   - **Key Point**: Yelling or walking out escalates conflict and stress.

   - **Technique**: Maintain a calm, controlled tone, even if the other person is upset. Practice *"seeking to understand rather than to be understood."*

Worksheet for Practice

Use this worksheet to **strengthen** your mind using the D-BELLS approach. Adapt it to fit your personal goals and daily routine.

1. **Identify Your Biggest Challenge**

   - Write down the primary issue: *Overthinking? Multitasking? Feeling overwhelmed?*

   - Note how often it occurs (e.g., daily, a few times a week).

2. **Pick One D-BELLS Element to Focus On**

   - **D (Kindness)**: How can you incorporate at least one act of kindness today?

   - **B (Patience)**: What trigger situation can you approach with calm instead of frustration?

   - **E (Escape Sarcasm)**: When do you usually make snarky comments? Commit to avoiding them.

   - **L (Leave Early for Work)**: List steps to leave 10–15 minutes earlier.

   - **L (Leave Work at Work)**: Write down a simple after-work ritual (e.g., turning off notifications).

   - **S (Sort Out Differences)**: Identify a recent conflict. Plan how to discuss it calmly next time.

3. **Set a Daily or Weekly Goal**

   - Example: *"This week, I will leave for work 10 minutes early every day."*

   - Or: *"Each time I feel annoyed, I will pause and take a deep breath before responding."*

4. **Reflect Each Evening**

   - Did you meet your goal? If yes, how did it feel? If not, what got in the way?

   - Write down **one positive** outcome or moment of insight from practicing your chosen D-BELLS element.

5. **Adjust & Evolve**

- After a few days, consider trying another D-BELLS element.

- Over time, you'll build **mental muscle** across multiple areas—kindness, patience, stress management, and healthier boundaries.

A Positive Note to End On

By incorporating **D-BELLS** into your daily life, you're actively strengthening your mind—just as you would tone your muscles with dumbbells. Remember, **"Seek to understand rather than be understood, and be reflective in life."** Each act of kindness, each moment of patience, and each effort to leave work at work contributes to a **more balanced, resilient**, and **fulfilled** self.

Activity 11: Designing Tiny Habits

Disclaimer

- This exercise is designed for **mild lifestyle and behavioral challenges**—similar to tending to a small cut or scrape.

- If you are experiencing severe distress, suicidal thoughts, or any urgent mental health concern, please seek **professional help immediately**.

- These methods are intended to **complement**, not replace, therapy, counseling, or medical intervention.

Introduction: "Designing a Habit Is Like Growing a Plant"

When we establish new habits, we're essentially **planting** and **nurturing** seeds of change. Much like growing a tiny sprout, a well-designed habit requires **proper soil** (environment), **light and moisture** (time and resources), and regular **nourishment** (reinforcement) to take root.

3 Steps to Grow Your Habit Plant

1. Select a Seed or Sprout (Something TINY)

2. Choose Proper Soil, Light, Moisture, Place (Find a PERFECT SPOT)

3. Nourish Your Tiny Plant (Help the ROOTS Get Established)

Applying This to Habit Design

Step 1: Identify/Select a Tiny Behavior

1. **Starter Step + Tiny Behavior**

Example:

- Starter Step: *Take out the exercise mat.*

- Tiny Behavior: *Do 4 pushups.*

The starter step is something **super small** and easy, ensuring there's minimal resistance to getting started.

Step 2: Find a Good Spot (Anchor)

1. **Where Does the Tiny Behavior Fit Naturally in Your Day?**

   - Attach the **new tiny habit** to an **existing routine**—this existing routine becomes your **anchor**.

   - **Example**: After reading the newspaper, you immediately do 4 pushups.

2. **Why an Anchor?**

   - Anchors leverage **established habits**, ensuring you won't "forget" your new habit.

   - It's easier to **remember** when you slot the new habit into a **specific**, pre-existing time or activity.

Step 3: Design Your Habit

1. **Pair the Tiny Behavior with a Good Anchor**

   - Use the formula: After I [existing anchor], I will [new tiny behavior].\text{After I [existing anchor], I will [new tiny behavior].}After I [existing anchor], I will [new tiny behavior].

- **Example:**

  - *After I read the newspaper (anchor), I will do 4 pushups (tiny behavior).*

2. **Nourishing Your Tiny Behavior**

- Celebrate **small wins**. Each time you follow through, acknowledge it—whether by a mental "good job!" or a mini reward.

- Over time, these **tiny actions** will solidify into **firmly established** habits.

Worksheet for Practice

Use this worksheet to **design** your new tiny habit, mirroring the planting process.

1. **Choose Your Tiny Behavior**

- Write down a **starter step** (e.g., *Take out my yoga mat*) and the **tiny behavior** itself (e.g., *Do 2 minutes of stretching* or *4 pushups*).

2. **Identify Your Anchor**

- List **3 daily habits** you already do without fail (e.g., *brushing teeth, making coffee, reading the newspaper*).

- Which of these fits **best** with your new tiny behavior?

3. **Create Your Statement**

- Use the formula: After I [existing anchor], I will [new tiny behavior].\text{After I [existing anchor], I will [new tiny behavior].}After I [existing anchor], I will [new tiny behavior].

- Example:

  - *After I drink my morning coffee, I will do 4 pushups.*

4. **Implement & Track**

   - For the next **7 days**, do this habit **immediately** after your anchor.

   - Each evening, note whether you **completed** the habit.

5. **Reflect & Adjust**

   - If it's not sticking, consider if you need a **smaller** behavior or a **different** anchor.

   - Success is more likely when the habit is **tiny** and **pairs** well with something you already do.

6. **Celebrate Progress**

   - Even if it's just **one pushup**, **one minute**, or **one new habit—** take a moment to appreciate the effort.

   - Over time, **tiny** habits can **grow** into major transformations.

A Positive Note to End On

Designing tiny habits is akin to nurturing **small seeds** until they take root. With **consistency** and **celebration**, these minuscule shifts can grow into **strong, life-changing routines**—just like the gradual unveiling of deeper truths in *Decoding Mithya*. Step by step, day by day, watch your new habits **flourish** into a healthier, more fulfilling lifestyle.

Activity 12: The Power of Colours (Colorology)

Disclaimer

- This exercise is designed for **mild emotional challenges**—similar to tending to a small cut or scrape.

- If you are experiencing severe distress, suicidal thoughts, or any urgent mental health concern, please seek **professional help immediately**.

- These methods are intended to **complement**, not replace, therapy, counseling, or medical intervention.

Introduction: Colours That Define Us

We often introduce ourselves with simple facts—our name, where we live, or our favourite colour. But **why** do we choose a particular colour as our favourite, and **how** does it shape our experiences? Colours can evoke **joy**, **sadness**, **hope**, and a variety of emotional states. They not only change our mood but also influence **stress levels**, **energy**, and even **creativity**.

In alternative therapies—like **feng shui**, **acupuncture**, or **chromotherapy**—colours and light are integral to promoting **physical**, **mental**, **emotional**, and **spiritual** well-being.

Life Challenges

This activity is especially helpful if you're dealing with:

- **Low Focus**

- **Anxiety**

- **Stress**

- **Negative Overthinking**

Colorology: Understanding How Colours Affect Us

Colours can produce different physical, emotional, and psychological effects. Surrounding yourself with **"the right"** colours can help reduce anxiety and stress while boosting mood and concentration.

Common Colours and Their Effects

1. **Red**

   - **Impact**: Exciting and stimulating.

   - **Use Case**: If you're in an emotional slump, **red** can help lift your spirits.

   - **Caution**: Too much red can be overwhelming.

2. **Pink**

   - **Impact**: Soft, tranquil, promotes peace and balance.

   - **Use Case**: Ideal when seeking calmness or a gentle emotional atmosphere.

3. **Orange**

   - **Impact**: Intense, invigorating, stimulating.

   - **Use Case**: Helpful for boosting energy and enthusiasm.

4. **Yellow**

   - **Impact**: Sunny, cheerful, mood-lifting.

- **Use Case**: Helpful in counteracting stress or negativity.

5. **Green**

   - **Impact**: Quiet, restful, soothing.

   - **Use Case**: Can diffuse anxiety and invite harmony.

6. **Blue**

   - **Impact**: Peaceful, calming, stress-reducing.

   - **Use Case**: Encourages a powerful sense of calm and helps with stress management.

7. **Purple**

   - **Impact**: Symbolizes strength, wisdom, and peace.

   - **Use Case**: Invokes tranquillity and can help reduce stress.

8. **White**

   - **Impact**: Purity, freshness, mental clarity.

   - **Use Case**: Bright white can inspire clarity, but dull white might cloud emotions.

9. **Black**

   - **Impact**: Represents power or submission, depending on context.

   - **Use Case**: Use sparingly, as it can encourage extremes or feel too heavy.

Colours and Memory

The colours we use while studying or recalling information can significantly affect **memory retention** and **focus**.

- **Orange, Red, Yellow**: Attention-grabbing—use for highlighting or underlining key concepts.

- **Red**: Draws attention; good for memory retrieval.

- **Yellow**: Stimulates mental activity; helps keep you alert.

- **Blue**: Boosts creative thinking.

- **Blue & Green**: Calming colours that can **increase concentration** and reduce mental fatigue.

Worksheet for Practice

1. **Colour Awareness Exercise**

   a. **Identify Your Go-To Colours**

      - Think about the colours you naturally gravitate toward in your clothing, workspace, or home decor.

      - Write them down: *Which colours appear most in your environment?*

   b. **Observe Emotional Responses**

      - For each colour you noted, ask: *How do I feel when I see this colour?*

      - Example: *"Red energizes me," "Green relaxes me," "Pink makes me feel calm."*

2. Colour Mood Board

a. Create a Visual Mood Board

- Gather items or images (online or physical) representing the colours you'd like to incorporate more intentionally.

- Arrange them in a collage or a digital board to see how they **interact**.

b. Analyse Your Selections

- Does your board lean towards **cool**, **warm**, **bright**, or **neutral** tones?

- Reflect on how this palette could support your **current emotional needs** (e.g., more calm if you're stressed, more stimulation if you're feeling low).

3. Study or Work Setup

a. Highlight Key Points

- Experiment with different **highlight colours** for your notes.

- See if using **red** or **orange** for critical data improves your recall or **blue** for more creative thinking tasks.

b. Set a Colourful Ambience

- Add a **plant** (green) or a **lamp** with a coloured bulb (blue or yellow) to your workspace.

- Note any changes in your **focus**, **mood**, or **productivity** over a week.

4. Daily Colour Check-In

a. Morning Routine

- Choose one colour to **wear** or **visualize** each day that aligns with how you want to feel.

- Example: *Wear a bright yellow accessory on a day you need extra optimism.*

b. Evening Reflection

- Journal about whether that colour had any impact on your **emotions** or **stress levels**.

A Positive Note to End On

Colours are woven into the fabric of our daily lives, often **subconsciously** influencing how we **feel**, **think**, and **act**. By learning to **harness** their power—whether it's to lift your mood, calm your mind, or sharpen your focus—you're taking another step toward a more **intentional** and **self-aware** life. Much like revealing deeper truths in *Decoding Mithya*, exploring colour can unlock new layers of **self-discovery** and **well-being**.

Activity 13: Fruitology Techniques – WATERMELON & MANGO Therapy

Disclaimer

- This exercise is designed for **mild stress and emotional challenges**—similar to tending to a small cut or scrape.

- If you are experiencing severe distress, suicidal thoughts, or any urgent mental health concern, please seek **professional help immediately**.

- These methods are intended to **complement**, not replace, therapy, counseling, or medical intervention.

Introduction: "Stress—Wanting to Be 'There' Instead of 'Here'"

Stress often arises from the **inner chatter** in our mind—our body's **fight-or-flight** response to perceived threats or demands. Unchecked, it can spiral into **anxiety**. But stress, in itself, isn't the villain; our reaction is. Embracing strategies to **manage** stress can transform our mindset and improve well-being.

Fruitology Techniques: Like a refreshing slice of watermelon, we can "cool down" stress. Meanwhile, MANGO therapy reminds us to keep **calm** and focus on simple, uplifting actions.

Life Challenges

This activity is especially helpful if you're dealing with:

- **Overthinking**

- **Feeling Overburdened**

- **Struggling with Stress and Anxiety**

Part A: WATERMELON – Cool as a Summer Fruit

"Be as Cool As WATERMELON"

W – Water Therapy

- **Stay Hydrated**: Dehydration worsens stress. Keep a water bottle close by.

- **Breathing & Bathing**: Take regular baths (maybe with aroma oils) to relax body and mind.

- **Fun Fact**: Under stress, heart rate and breathing increase, leading to fluid loss—so drink up!

A – Ability to Bounce Back

- **Resilience**: The capacity to adapt to obstacles.

- **Ways to Build Resilience**:

  1. Stop viewing crises as challenges to avoid.

  2. Cultivate a strong support system.

  3. Accept change as a natural part of life.

  4. Embrace self-discovery.

  5. Maintain a positive outlook about self and strengths.

T – Time Management

- **Prioritize Tasks**: Use to-do lists with levels of urgency.

- **Pareto Principle (80/20 Rule)**: Focus energy on the 20% of work yielding 80% of the results.

- **Structure**: Plan your day, get up early, manage productive vs. unproductive time.

E – Exercise Regularly

- **Sitting = The New Smoking**: Move your body to reduce stress.

- **Ideas**: Yoga, cardio, skipping rope—even at home if external circumstances limit outdoor activities.

R – Rhythmic Breathing

- **Calm Your Nerves**: Stress affects thinking and breathing.

- **4-7-8 Technique**: Inhale for 4 seconds, hold for 7, exhale for 8.

- **Benefit**: Slows heart rate and quiets the mind.

M – ME Time

- **Set Aside 30 Minutes** daily just for yourself.

- **Engage in Passions**: Painting, dancing, cooking, or any hobby.

- **Know Your Stress Meter**: Step back or "cool down" before burnout.

E – Eat Healthy, Well-Balanced Diet

- **Meals**: Include vegetables, fruits, whole grains, lean protein—no skipping!

- **Mind Power**: Good nutrition boosts mental energy; poor diet drains it.

- **Bonus**: Healthy eating doubles as a stress management tool.

L – Learn to Take Breaks

- **Avoid Overloading**: Don't put too many tasks in one basket.

- **Prioritize**: Tackle urgent tasks first.

- **Mini Breaks**: Even 1–2 minutes to stand up and stretch can recharge your mind and body.

O – Organized

- **Declutter**: Physical clutter adds to mental stress.

- **Minimalist Study/Work Area**: Freed of distractions, you can focus better.

- **Delete Unwanted Stuff**: Like removing spam from an inbox, clear out negative thoughts and clutter.

N – Need of EQ (Emotional Quotient)

- **Manage Emotions**: Uncontrolled emotions lead to stress and relationship problems.

- **Understand Your Feelings**: Self-awareness helps you express them healthily.

- **So**: *Understand Emotions – Rationalize – Practice*

Part B: MANGO Therapy – Keep CALM & Eat AAM

M – Music Therapy

- **Stress Reliever**: Music calms nerves and stimulates the mind.

- **Ideas**: Soothing music or upbeat tunes for a quick pick-me-up.

- **For Kids**: Background classical or instrumental can aid studying or relaxation.

A – Affirmations and Positive Attitude

- **Train Your Brain**: Replace negative self-talk with uplifting thoughts.

- **Glass Half Full**: Challenge yourself to find a positive angle.

- **Action Steps**:

  1. Identify negative thoughts/behaviors you want to change.

  2. Craft realistic, positive statements that oppose them.

  3. Repeat these affirmations throughout the day.

N – NO (Art of Saying NO)

1. **Simple Response**: Be firm, direct. Remember, you don't need permission to say NO.

2. **Buy Time**: Don't commit on the spot; think over your options.

3. **No Guilt**: Sometimes it's beneficial for others (including children) to hear "NO."

4. **Stay True to Yourself**: Be clear about what you actually want.

G – Get Enough Sleep

- **Happiness = Good Rest**: 7–9 hours recommended for young adults and adults.

- **Power Naps**: Short rests can be refreshing.

- **Learning & Stress**: Adequate sleep improves memory and lowers stress.

O – SMILE

- **Free Therapy**: Smiling reduces the body's stress response.

- **Physical Benefits**: Can lower heart rate during stressful moments.

- **Trick the Brain**: Smiling convinces your mind you're happy, even if you weren't initially.

Worksheet for Practice: Fruitology Stress-Busting

1. **WATERMELON Check-In**

   - **Which letter resonates most** with your current stress? (W, A, T, E, R, M, E, L, O, N)

   - **One Action**: Choose **one** strategy (e.g., practicing "ME time" daily or trying "Time Management" with the 80/20 rule).

2. **MANGO Check-In**

   - Pick **one** therapy aspect to focus on (Music, Affirmations, NO, Get Enough Sleep, Smile).

- **Implementation Plan**: For instance, if you choose "NO," list **two** scenarios where you'll stand firm this week.

3. **Set Mini Goals**

   - **Example**: "I will do the 4-7-8 breathing exercise twice a day" or "I will go to bed by 10 pm on weekdays."

4. **Journal**

   - End each day by noting how effectively you used the chosen strategies.

   - Were there obstacles? How did you overcome them (or not)?

5. **Reflect & Reward**

   - After a week, evaluate any **improvements** in mood, stress levels, or overall energy.

   - Celebrate small successes—treat yourself to a favorite snack or activity.

A Positive Note to End On

Embracing **WATERMELON** and **MANGO** therapies is like keeping a refreshing slice of fruit close at hand—simple, nurturing, and revitalizing. Each letter offers a practical, bite-sized way to tackle stress and cultivate well-being. Much like the deeper self-discovery in *Decoding Mithya*, these Fruitology techniques remind us that **small, consistent steps** can lead to significant breakthroughs in managing stress and thriving in our daily lives.

Activity 14: HOPE – The Gift That Changes Everything

Disclaimer

- This exercise is designed for **mild emotional challenges**—similar to tending to a small cut or scrape.

- If you are experiencing severe distress, suicidal thoughts, or any urgent mental health concern, please seek **professional help immediately**.

- These methods are intended to **complement**, not replace, therapy, counseling, or medical intervention.

Introduction: HOPE Changes Everything

Hope is the **invisible thread** that keeps us moving forward, even when faced with negative life events, loss, or grief. Consciously or unconsciously, hope shapes the **narrative** of our lives—defining our desires for the future and fueling our belief that we can overcome challenges.

Life Challenges

This activity is especially helpful if you're dealing with:

- **Negative Life Events**

- **Life Dissatisfaction**

- **Personal or Material Loss**

- **Grief**

Pause & Think

- Can you remember the **best gift** you ever received?

- Was it for a birthday, a festival, or a random surprise?

- Do you recall who gave it to you?

The one **gift** that often goes unrecognized yet stands out for a lifetime is the **"Gift of Hope."** Sadly, many of us don't realize its power because we tend to **choose fear** or remain afraid instead of embracing hope.

So, why not **gift yourself** this precious treasure?

"Hope audaciously. Others can give you statistics, predictions, and probabilities, but only you can decide what to hope for. So decide."

—Wendy Edey

H.O.P.E. Framework

H – HONESTY

- **Speak Truthfully**: Be honest in what you say to **others** and, more importantly, to **yourself**.

- **Encouraging Self-Talk**:

  - *"I learn from mistakes."*

  - *"I can accomplish anything."*

  - *"I can do difficult tasks."*

  - *"I like celebrating my own growth."*

Why Honesty Matters

When we **deny** our feelings or **hide** from our fears, we push hope away. Embracing **honesty** builds a strong foundation for true self-belief.

O – OPTIMISM

- **Choose a Positive Lens**: Being a pessimist rarely changes the world—but an **optimistic** outlook can.

- **Action Step**: Each morning, list **one thing** you're looking forward to. It can be as simple as enjoying a warm meal or calling a friend.

Small Shifts, Big Impact

Optimism **doesn't** mean ignoring problems. It's about believing that **solutions** and **better outcomes** are possible.

P – PRIDE & PEACE

1. **Pride in Little Accomplishments**

   o Celebrate small milestones; each one **accumulates** into something bigger.

   o Example: *Finishing a short workout or learning a new recipe might seem minor, but it builds self-trust.*

2. **Be at PEACE with Yourself**

   o Cultivate **calm** and **contentment** through reflective practices (meditation, journaling, or simply a quiet walk).

- o Peace allows **hope** to grow without the noise of self-criticism.

E – ENCOURAGEMENT

- **Self-Encouragement = Self-Motivation**: Don't wait for external validation.

- **Practical Tips:**

  1. **Mindful of Small Wins**: Acknowledge each step forward.

  2. **Celebrate Achievements**: Reward yourself, even if it's just a mental pat on the back.

  3. **Believe in "I Can"**: Keep a list of personal affirmations.

  4. **Positive Influences**: Surround yourself with supportive people or uplifting content.

  5. **Be Open to Learning**: Mistakes are opportunities for growth.

Worksheet for Practice: The HOPE Gift

1. **Gift to Yourself**

   - o Write down **three statements** of honesty about your current situation or emotions.

   - o For each statement, note **one step** you can take to improve or address it.

2. **Daily Optimism Check**

   o   In a journal or on your phone, record **one thing** that brings you **hope** each day (e.g., a sunrise, a supportive friend, a new goal).

3. **Celebrate Small Wins (Pride & Peace)**

   o   **Weekly Tally**: List **5 small achievements** (e.g., "I organized my desk," "I called an old friend," "I tried a new recipe").

   o   Reflect on how these minor accomplishments contribute to **peace of mind**.

4. **Self-Encouragement Plan**

   o   **Action**: Choose **one** affirmation (e.g., "I am capable and resilient") and repeat it **three times** a day—morning, noon, and night.

   o   **Record**: Note any changes in mood or motivation after **one week**.

5. **HOPE Anchor**

   o   Combine honesty and optimism into a **single** anchor statement.

   o   Example: *"I am honest about my struggles, but hopeful about my abilities to overcome them."*

   o   Place this statement where you'll see it daily (mirror, phone wallpaper, desk).

A Positive Note to End On

Hope is more than a wish; it's the fuel that **drives** us forward when circumstances feel dire. By embracing **HONESTY, OPTIMISM, PRIDE & PEACE**, and **ENCOURAGEMENT**, you gift yourself an **inner compass** that points toward better days. Like the journey in *Decoding Mithya*, **HOPE** helps us shed fear and discover our **innate strength**. Trust this gift—it can truly **change everything**.

Activity 15: Time for Exam Myth Buster

Disclaimer

- This exercise is designed for **mild academic and exam-related challenges**—similar to tending to a small cut or scrape.

- If you are experiencing severe distress, panic attacks, or any urgent mental health concern, please seek **professional help immediately**.

- These methods are intended to **complement**, not replace, therapy, counseling, or medical intervention.

Introduction: Exam Fever—Myth vs. Reality

Even the brightest minds—Albert Einstein and Winston Churchill—faced what we colloquially term "exam fever." Whether you're a top student or just getting by, the pressure of exams can stir **anxiety**, **performance stress**, and even **fear**. By busting some common myths, you can approach exam preparation and test-taking with a **calmer**, more **confident** mindset.

Life Challenges

This activity is especially helpful if you're dealing with:

- **Exam Fever**

- **Test Phobia**

- **Low Motivation**

- **Performance Anxiety**

- **Parental Pressure**

- **Peer Pressure**

Exam Fundamentals: Two Key Parts

1. **Exam Savvy**

   o Understanding **test formats, time management**, and **question strategies.**

2. **Anxiety Management**

   o Calming the **mind and body** so you can recall information clearly and stay **organized.**

Myths vs. Facts

Myth 1: "Only academically weak students get nervous."

- **Fact:** Anyone—regardless of academic strength—can experience **stress** and **nervousness.**

- **Reality:** Even toppers may have strong stress symptoms.

Myth 2: "Some students are naturally good at studying."

- **Fact:** Effective study skills can be **learned** by anyone.

- **Reality:** Techniques like **note-taking, spacing,** and **active recall** help all learners.

Myth 3: "Morning is the best time to study."

- **Fact:** Personal preference rules. Some people focus better **early;** others are **night owls.**

- **Reality**: Honor your **natural rhythms** for maximum retention.

Myth 4: "More hours studying = higher marks."

- **Fact**: It's about **quality**, not just **quantity**.

- **Reality**: Strategic study (e.g., spaced repetition, targeted practice) often beats marathon sessions.

Myth 5: "Reading the entire question paper at once is essential."

- **Fact**: If reading everything at once causes **anxiety**, you can tackle questions **one by one**.

- **Reality**: Skip or leave space for questions you don't know—come back later.

Myth 6: "Ignoring exam anxiety will make it disappear."

- **Fact**: Avoidance can worsen stress, leading to physical and emotional strain.

- **Reality**: Acknowledge anxiety and take **positive steps** to manage it (breathing exercises, breaks, etc.).

Myth 7: "Willpower and intelligence eliminate exam anxiety."

- **Fact**: IQ and **willpower** don't guarantee freedom from stress.

- **Reality**: Exam anxiety can affect **anyone**, regardless of age, background, or ability.

Key Takeaway

Exam anxiety **does not** discriminate. It hits anyone, regardless of **IQ, socioeconomic status,** or **academic ability**. Mastering **mindset**

techniques, **calming emotions**, and **relaxation** strategies puts you into the **Exam Zone**: a clear, focused state where **memory recall** and **mental alertness** thrive.

"Trust yourself; you know more than you think you do."

Worksheet for Practice: Busting Exam Myths

1. **Identify Your Beliefs**

   o List 2–3 **myths** you subconsciously believe about exams or test-taking.

   o Example: "I must study 10 hours a day to do well."

2. **Rewrite the Myths as Facts**

   o Turn each myth into a **positive, evidence-based statement**.

   o Example: "Quality of study techniques is more crucial than total hours studied."

3. **Personalize Your Study Routine**

   o **Choose Your Best Time**: Morning, afternoon, or night—select what **truly** works for you.

   o **Strategize**: Plan how you'll study (short bursts, spaced repetition, or group study).

4. **Anxiety-Busting Techniques**

   o **Breathing Exercise**: 4-7-8 method or simple deep breaths when feeling overwhelmed.

- ○ **Mindful Breaks**: Take 5-minute walks or do light stretches to reset between study blocks.

- ○ **Visualization**: Picture yourself confidently walking into the exam hall, calm and prepared.

5. **Reflect & Adjust**

- ○ After trying these strategies for a week, note **what improved** and **where you still struggle**.

- ○ **Tweak** your routine, study method, or anxiety management as needed.

A Positive Note to End On

Exams are temporary—but the **mindset** and **skills** you build now can last a lifetime. By **debunking myths** and **adopting practical strategies**, you shift from a place of fear to one of **confidence**. Much like unlearning outdated societal myths in *Decoding Mithya*, confronting exam myths frees you to **perform at your best**—calm, focused, and ready to showcase what you know.

Activity 16: Do's and Don'ts for Parents of Teens

Disclaimer

- This exercise is designed for **mild parenting and communication challenges**—similar to tending to a small cut or scrape.

- If you are experiencing severe distress, family crises, or any urgent mental health concern, please seek **professional help immediately**.

- These methods are intended to **complement**, not replace, therapy, counseling, or medical intervention.

Introduction: Bridging the Gap with Teens

Parenting adolescents can feel like walking a tightrope—managing **fixed mindsets**, **power struggles**, or **helicopter tendencies** while trying not to push them away. Whether it's over-involvement in school, prying at home, or inadvertently nagging, parents sometimes struggle to strike a balance. This activity provides straightforward **do's and don'ts** both at **school** and **home** to help foster empathy, respect, and open communication with teens.

Life Challenges

This activity is especially helpful if you're dealing with:

- **Fixed Mindset**

- **Power Trip**

- **Helicopter Parenting**

- **Habit of Pestering**

- **Spying**

1. Do's & Don'ts at the School Level

Do's

1. **A – Accept & Acknowledge Their Little Efforts**

   ○ Recognize and praise even minor achievements.

   ○ This builds confidence and encourages them to keep trying.

2. **B – Be Patient**

   ○ Adolescents are still developing emotionally and cognitively.

   ○ Patience teaches them resilience and self-compassion.

3. **C – Cultivate Empathy**

   ○ Encourage teens to consider others' perspectives.

   ○ Model empathetic behavior to help them handle conflicts and stress.

Don'ts

1. **Stop Grading Them**

   ○ Avoid labeling or constantly comparing them to peers or siblings.

   ○ Let them know they're more than just "marks" or a "score."

2. **Stop Assumption & Don't Judge**

   - Don't assume their reasons or motives without listening first.

   - Create a safe space for honest communication.

3. **Stop Criticizing & Advising All the Time**

   - Continuous criticism can undermine their self-esteem.

   - Offer guidance sparingly and let them learn from experience.

2. Do's & Don'ts at the Home Level

Do's

1. **Connection**

   - Use family mealtimes to **connect** and share daily stories.

   - Prioritize face-to-face conversations to strengthen bonds.

2. **Change with Time**

   - Embrace an **open mind**. The digital and social media world can be overwhelming for teens.

   - Keep learning about new trends or apps they use.

3. **TALK & LISTEN**

   - Listen deeply and discuss issues with your teen.

   - Share your perspective in a mutually respectful way.

   - Encouragement and praise really matter to them—say it often.

Don'ts

1. **Over-Regulation (Helicopter Parenting)**

   o   Avoid micromanaging your teen's every move.

   o   Empower them to make some decisions on their own.

2. **Control Your Response**

   o   When provoked, respond calmly rather than reacting with anger or fear.

   o   Overreactions can push teens into hiding important details.

3. **Don't Be Shocked**

   o   Be open-minded about what your teen shares.

   o   If you seem shocked, they may hesitate to come to you in a crisis.

4. **Don't Try to Change Them**

   o   Guide them gently rather than forcibly molding them.

   o   Acknowledge their individuality.

3. Strict No-No (Don'ts): "How Much Is Too Much?"

1. **"Let's Talk"—Stay Away**

   o   **Parents**: "Let's talk" seems harmless.

   o   **Teens**: Alarm bells go off; they sense a lecture coming. Conversation ends before it begins.

- o **Solution**: Spend **non-demanding** time first. Read a book in the same room or help them with a chore. Then ease into the conversation.

2. **Stop Preaching**

   - o **Parents**: We often default to telling teens what to do—"Study," "Sit properly," "Behave!"

   - o **Teens**: They may "push back" when constantly told or instructed.

   - o **Solution**: Replace "You need to study" with "How's your exam prep going?" Ask with **curiosity** and calmness.

3. **Keep Calm**

   - o **Parents**: If your teen says, "I messed up," avoid responding with "I told you so!"

   - o **Teens**: They'll think twice before confiding in you again.

   - o **Solution**: Empathize with an open heart: *"That sounds tough. I'm here for you."*

4. **Follow the YOU–I–WE Approach**

   - o **YOU**: "I listen to you (even if I don't agree)."

   - o **I**: "I share my views (even if you don't agree)."

   - o **WE**: "We solve it together."

   - o This approach fosters collaboration and mutual respect.

5. **Learn to Say SORRY**

   o Parents aren't perfect. If you've made a mistake, own up to it.

   o Teens are surprisingly forgiving when you're honest and sincere: *"I'm sorry for messing up. How can I make it better?"*

Worksheet for Practice: Building Better Parent-Teen Relations

1. **Identify One Habit to Change**

   o E.g., micromanaging homework, reacting immediately to mistakes, or using "Let's talk" to start every conversation.

2. **Plan a "Non-Demanding" Activity**

   o Choose a simple task: cooking together, short walk, or quiet reading in the same room.

   o Practice gentle conversation starters afterward.

3. **Apply the YOU–I–WE Model**

   o Write one scenario (e.g., disagreement about curfew) and script how you'll handle it using **YOU–I–WE**.

4. **Reflect on Reactions**

   o Track your emotional response when a teen shares something shocking or negative.

   o Note how

   o you managed it: Did you keep calm, show empathy?

5. **Apologize When Needed**

   o   If a conflict arises, consider offering a genuine apology.

   o   Record how your teen responds and how it shifts the dynamic.

A Positive Note to End On

Parenting teens doesn't have to be a battleground. By **communicating with empathy**, offering gentle guidance, and admitting when you've erred, you pave the way for a stronger, more trusting relationship. Much like the lessons in *Decoding Mithya*, this process involves unlearning old habits and adopting a more **mindful, respectful** approach—one that acknowledges the unique journey of both parent and adolescent.

Activity 17: Sleep Diaries 2 — Self-Revenge

Disclaimer

- This exercise is designed for **mild habit and lifestyle challenges**—similar to tending to a small cut or scrape.

- If you are experiencing severe insomnia, anxiety, depression, or any urgent mental health concern, please seek **professional help immediately**.

- These methods are intended to **complement**, not replace, therapy, counseling, or medical intervention.

Introduction: The Revenge Bedtime Procrastination (RBP) Phenomenon

Do you find yourself scrolling endlessly at midnight, even though you're exhausted? This may be a sign of **Revenge Bedtime Procrastination**—the habit of staying up late to reclaim "me time" after a hectic day. While not all late-night activity is harmful, deliberately postponing sleep can lead to **less sleep, fatigue**, and a **negative impact** on well-being. This activity explores how to identify RBP, address underlying emotions, and nurture healthier sleep habits.

Life Challenges

This activity is especially helpful if you're dealing with:

- **Lack of Motivation**

- **Negative Emotion**

- **Resentment**

1. Understanding Revenge Bedtime Procrastination (RBP)

1. **Definition**

   - "Revenge Bedtime Procrastination" is staying up late to gain personal time, despite knowing you should be sleeping. It's a self-revenge against a jam-packed schedule.

2. **Signs**

   - **Compromised Sleep Hours**: Delayed bedtime, resulting in consistently less sleep.

   - **Non-Medical Reason**: Postponing sleep for reasons other than illness or environmental disruptions.

   - **Awareness of Harm**: You know it impacts your health, yet you continue.

3. **Not Always Harmful**

   - Late nights can be productive or part of a normal schedule if you **still get adequate rest**. RBP becomes problematic when it cuts into essential sleep.

2. ABC… to STOP Procrastination

1. **A – Adding Time Delay**

   - Introduce a **brief pause** before you cave into late-night distractions.

   - Example: Count backward from 10 or try a short mindfulness exercise to curb the urge.

2. **B – Bedtime Routine**

   o Create a **calming routine**: Light music, meditation, or reading something soothing.

   o If certain daytime activities leave you unhappy, learn to **let them go** instead of ruminating at night.

3. **C – Changing Environment**

   o Minimize **exposure to bright lights** before bedtime.

   o Keep electronic devices away—no doom-scrolling or streaming in bed.

3. Bad Sleep Habits to Sleep Hygiene

1. **Limit Naps**

   o Reduce or avoid daytime naps that interfere with nighttime sleep.

   o Keep a **consistent sleep schedule** (same bedtime and wake time).

2. **Healthy Pre-Bed Habits**

   o Avoid **heavy meals**, **caffeine**, and **blue light** (from phones/tablets) close to bedtime.

   o Replace negative bedtime routines with **relaxation exercises**—like gentle stretches or journaling.

3. **Sleep Is Important**

   o Remind yourself daily: Adequate sleep improves mood, concentration, and overall health.

- Tweak your environment to encourage sleep (comfortable bedding, cool room temperature, etc.).

4. Changing Habits

1. **Separate Sleep Space**

   - Use your bedroom **primarily for sleeping**. Avoid working, watching TV, or eating in bed.

   - This trains your brain to associate the bedroom with rest.

2. **Early Night Routine**

   - Set an **alarm one hour** before your usual bedtime to start winding down.

   - Use this hour for a warm bath, calming music, or light reading—anything that soothes.

3. **Exercise & Daylight**

   - Getting **morning sunlight** and daily physical activity can help regulate your circadian rhythm.

   - Even a brief walk outside can help you feel more tired at night.

4. **Be Kind to Yourself**

   - Recognize your emotions without judgment.

   - Accept your feelings of resentment, stress, or exhaustion, and address them during the day instead of at bedtime.

Worksheet for Practice: Building Better Sleep Habits

1. **Identify One Late-Night Trigger**

   o E.g., scrolling social media, binge-watching TV, or snacking.

   o Write down when it typically happens and why.

2. **Plan a Substitute Activity**

   o Replace the trigger with a **calming alternative** (e.g., reading 10 pages of a book, listening to instrumental music).

   o Set a **time limit** (e.g., 15 minutes) before lights out.

3. **Set a Bedtime Alarm**

   o Decide on a **realistic** bedtime.

   o An hour before that, set an alarm to remind yourself it's **wind-down time**.

   o Note how it affects your willingness to stop revenge procrastination.

4. **Track Progress**

   • Maintain a **sleep diary** for a week, noting:

      o Nightly bedtime and wake-up time

      o Any leisure activities done before sleep

      o Overall mood and energy level the next day

5. **Reflect & Adjust**

   o   At the end of the week, review your diary.

   o   Did you reduce RBP episodes? Feel more rested?

   o   Tweak your routine based on what worked or didn't.

A Positive Note to End On

Reclaiming your nights doesn't mean giving up "me time"; it means **prioritizing** what truly helps you thrive. By addressing **negative emotions**, building a **healthy routine**, and treating yourself with **compassion**, you can transform late-night self-sabotage into restorative **sleep habits**. As with the self-discovery journey in *Decoding Mithya*, every small step toward mindfulness and self-care paves the way for a **more balanced, happier life**.

Activity 18: Circle of Life – Emotional & Mental Well-Being

Disclaimer

- This exercise is designed for **mild mental and emotional wellness challenges**—similar to tending to a small cut or scrape.

- If you are experiencing severe distress, recurring depression, anxiety disorders, or any urgent mental health concern, please seek **professional help immediately**.

- These methods are intended to **complement**, not replace, therapy, counseling, or medical intervention.

Introduction: Life Comes Full Circle

As **Leonardo da Vinci** said, "Realize that everything connects to everything else." Our lives indeed move in **circles**—moments of joy, moments of struggle, and moments of growth. Similarly, **Lord Shree Krishna** in the *Bhagavad Gita* reminds us that managing our mind is pivotal: "For one who has conquered his mind, a mind is the best of friends, but for one who has failed to do so, a mind is the greatest enemy." This activity focuses on recognizing the **ebb and flow** of emotions, practicing **self-care**, and embracing the concept that **nothing is permanent**.

Life Challenges

This activity is especially helpful if you're dealing with:

- **Negative Emotions** (Sadness, Anger, Jealousy)

- **Difficulty Coping with Day-to-Day Life**

- **Self-Care Deficits**

- **Unhealthy Attachments**

1. The Art of Managing Mental & Emotional Well-Being

1. **Definition**

   - Mental or emotional well-being doesn't mean perpetual **happiness**. It means being **aware** of emotions and having the **skills** to cope with life's ups and downs.

2. **Healthy vs. Unhealthy Emotions**

   - It's normal to feel **sadness**, **anxiety**, **anger**, or **jealousy**; these emotions alert and protect us.

   - Emotions become **unhealthy** when they are **excessive**, **irrational**, or **interfere** with daily functioning.

3. **Seeking Help**

   - If overwhelming emotions disrupt your **work, relationships,** or **self-care**, consider **professional support**.

2. The Need for Self-Care

1. **"Prevention is Better Than Cure"**

   - This applies as much to mental health as it does to physical health.

   - Self-care is how you **recharge** and **reclaim** your inner power.

2. **Mind-Aid Pitara Guide**

   - Explore **tips and techniques** for maintaining mental and emotional well-being.

   - Use self-care to **manage** stress before it escalates.

3. **Daily Self-Care Reminders**

   - Even **small acts** of self-care can anchor your mind during challenging times.

3. Self-Care @Happify Diary

Tips for Being Emotionally and Mentally Strong

- **Enjoy Your Company**: Spend time alone comfortably—learn who you are.

- **Stop Living in the Past**: Focus on the present and future solutions.

- **Stop Expecting Fast Results**: Real growth takes patience.

- **Don't Give Up After Failure**: Mistakes are stepping stones to success.

- **Stop Trying to Please Everyone**: You can't control others' reactions.

- **Learn to Say NO**: Boundaries are essential for well-being.

- **Learn to Take Responsibilities**: Own your actions without self-criticism.

- **Don't Let Others Influence Your Emotions**: Practice emotional independence.

- **Embrace Adversity**: "Nothing is permanent," even tough times pass.

- **Exercise Your Mind Daily**: Journaling, mindfulness, or problem-solving tasks.

- **Control Your Self-Talk**: Positive thoughts encourage resilience.

4. Positive Affirmations

1. **Mind Exercise**

   - Practice daily, ideally in front of a **mirror** or by journaling.

   - Choose **at least 5 affirmations** every day.

2. **Sample Affirmations**

   - "I am enough."

   - "I believe in my dreams."

   - "I love the way I am."

   - "My life is filled with an abundance of goodness."

   - "I am strong."

   - "I am worthy."

   - "I am kind."

   - "I am confident."

- (Feel free to add your own or tailor these to your needs.)

3. **Why Affirmations Work**

   - They **reframe** negative self-talk into uplifting statements.

   - Repetition helps solidify a **positive mindset** over time.

Worksheet for Practice: Circle of Emotional Well-Being

1. **Identify One Emotion Blocking Your Growth**

   - Write down the **emotion** (e.g., jealousy, resentment) and how often it appears.

2. **Self-Care Commitment**

   - Select **two activities** from the Self-Care @Happify list to practice this week.

   - Example: *"I will spend 10 minutes reading alone," "I will say NO to one request that stresses me."*

3. **Affirmation Routine**

   - Pick **5 affirmations** that resonate.

   - Recite them **every morning** or **every evening** in front of a mirror or in your journal.

   - Note any changes in your **mood** or **self-talk** after a week.

4. **Monitor Emotional Changes**

   - At the end of each day, jot down any significant **emotional reactions**.

- o See if the **frequency or intensity** of negative emotions is changing.

5. **Reflect & Adjust**

- After a week, reflect on your **progress**:

   - o Did self-care practices help?

   - o Did affirmations improve your self-image?

- Tweak your strategy based on what's working or not.

A Positive Note to End On

Like a circle, **life comes full circle**—today's challenges become tomorrow's lessons, and tomorrow's lessons become new chapters in your story. By **tuning** into your emotional and mental well-being, **taking charge** of self-care, and embracing daily affirmations, you set the stage for **healthier, more resilient living**. Much like the lessons in *Decoding Mithya*, remember that **every emotion** is a guide, and **every moment** is a chance to learn and grow.

Activity 19: Circle of Life – Emotional & Mental Well-Being

Disclaimer

- This exercise is designed for **mild mental and emotional wellness challenges**—similar to tending to a small cut or scrape.

- If you are experiencing severe distress, recurring depression, anxiety disorders, or any urgent mental health concern, please seek **professional help immediately**.

- These methods are intended to **complement**, not replace, therapy, counseling, or medical intervention.

Introduction: Life Comes Full Circle

As **Leonardo da Vinci** said, "Realize that everything connects to everything else." Our lives indeed move in **circles**—moments of joy, moments of struggle, and moments of growth. Similarly, **Lord Shree Krishna** in the *Bhagavad Gita* reminds us that managing our mind is pivotal: "For one who has conquered his mind, a mind is the best of friends, but for one who has failed to do so, a mind is the greatest enemy." This activity focuses on recognizing the **ebb and flow** of emotions, practicing **self-care**, and embracing the concept that **nothing is permanent**.

Life Challenges

This activity is especially helpful if you're dealing with:

- **Negative Emotions** (Sadness, Anger, Jealousy)

- **Difficulty Coping with Day-to-Day Life**

- **Self-Care Deficits**

- **Unhealthy Attachments**

1. The Art of Managing Mental & Emotional Well-Being

1. **Definition**

   - Mental or emotional well-being doesn't mean perpetual **happiness**. It means being **aware** of emotions and having the **skills** to cope with life's ups and downs.

2. **Healthy vs. Unhealthy Emotions**

   - It's normal to feel **sadness**, **anxiety**, **anger**, or **jealousy**; these emotions alert and protect us.

   - Emotions become **unhealthy** when they are **excessive**, **irrational**, or **interfere** with daily functioning.

3. **Seeking Help**

   - If overwhelming emotions disrupt your **work, relationships,** or **self-care**, consider **professional support**.

2. The Need for Self-Care

1. **"Prevention is Better Than Cure"**

   - This applies as much to mental health as it does to physical health.

   - Self-care is how you **recharge** and **reclaim** your inner power.

2. **Mind-Aid Pitara Guide**

- Explore **tips and techniques** for maintaining mental and emotional well-being.

- Use self-care to **manage** stress before it escalates.

3. **Daily Self-Care Reminders**

- Even **small acts** of self-care can anchor your mind during challenging times.

3. Self-Care @Happify Diary

Tips for Being Emotionally and Mentally Strong

- **Enjoy Your Company**: Spend time alone comfortably—learn who you are.

- **Stop Living in the Past**: Focus on the present and future solutions.

- **Stop Expecting Fast Results**: Real growth takes patience.

- **Don't Give Up After Failure**: Mistakes are stepping stones to success.

- **Stop Trying to Please Everyone**: You can't control others' reactions.

- **Learn to Say NO**: Boundaries are essential for well-being.

- **Learn to Take Responsibilities**: Own your actions without self-criticism.

- **Don't Let Others Influence Your Emotions**: Practice emotional independence.

- **Embrace Adversity**: "Nothing is permanent," even tough times pass.

- **Exercise Your Mind Daily**: Journaling, mindfulness, or problem-solving tasks.

- **Control Your Self-Talk**: Positive thoughts encourage resilience.

4. Positive Affirmations

1. **Mind Exercise**

   - Practice daily, ideally in front of a **mirror** or by journaling.

   - Choose **at least 5 affirmations** every day.

2. **Sample Affirmations**

   - "I am enough."

   - "I believe in my dreams."

   - "I love the way I am."

   - "My life is filled with an abundance of goodness."

   - "I am strong."

   - "I am worthy."

   - "I am kind."

   - "I am confident."

- (Feel free to add your own or tailor these to your needs.)

3. **Why Affirmations Work**

   - They **reframe** negative self-talk into uplifting statements.

   - Repetition helps solidify a **positive mindset** over time.

Worksheet for Practice: Circle of Emotional Well-Being

1. **Identify One Emotion Blocking Your Growth**

   - Write down the **emotion** (e.g., jealousy, resentment) and how often it appears.

2. **Self-Care Commitment**

   - Select **two activities** from the Self-Care @Happify list to practice this week.

   - Example: *"I will spend 10 minutes reading alone," "I will say NO to one request that stresses me."*

3. **Affirmation Routine**

   - Pick **5 affirmations** that resonate.

   - Recite them **every morning** or **every evening** in front of a mirror or in your journal.

   - Note any changes in your **mood** or **self-talk** after a week.

4. **Monitor Emotional Changes**

   - At the end of each day, jot down any significant **emotional reactions**.

- See if the **frequency or intensity** of negative emotions is changing.

5. **Reflect & Adjust**

- After a week, reflect on your **progress**:

    o Did self-care practices help?

    o Did affirmations improve your self-image?

- Tweak your strategy based on what's working or not.

Conclusion & Extra Tips

1. **Stay Curious**

- Life is a continuous loop of experiences—stay open to new ideas, learnings, and perspectives.

- Curiosity fosters adaptability and helps you bounce back from setbacks.

2. **Accept Impermanence**

- Remind yourself that feelings, challenges, and even victories are temporary.

- This mindset encourages detachment from negative events and humility in success.

3. **Celebrate Small Wins**

- Sometimes, progress is gradual. Give yourself credit for mini-achievements—finishing a journal entry, being mindful for five minutes, or saying NO in a difficult situation.

4. **Find Support**

- Connect with communities or individuals who share similar goals for mental and emotional well-being.

- Having an accountability partner—be it a friend, family member, or counselor—can keep you motivated.

5. **Iterate & Evolve**

- Don't be discouraged by slip-ups or slower progress.

- Evaluate your routines periodically and modify them to fit your current life situation.

A Positive Note to End On

Like a circle, **life comes full circle**—today's challenges become tomorrow's lessons, and tomorrow's lessons become new chapters in your story. By **tuning** into your emotional and mental well-being, **taking charge** of self-care, and embracing daily affirmations, you set the stage for **healthier, more resilient living**. Much like the lessons in *Decoding Mithya*, remember that **every emotion** is a guide, and **every moment** is a chance to learn and grow.

Activity 20: Take Care—Your Mental Well-Being Matters

Disclaimer

- This exercise is designed for **mild mental and emotional wellness challenges**—similar to tending to a small cut or scrape.

- If you are experiencing severe distress, recurring depression, anxiety disorders, or any urgent mental health concern, please seek **professional help immediately**.

- These methods are intended to **complement**, not replace, therapy, counseling, or medical intervention.

Introduction: Breaking the Taboo Around Mental Health

In this whirlwind of life, **self-awareness** is your anchor. **Talk** to the people who genuinely matter—friends, family, or a counselor. **Accept** that everyone faces challenges, and therapy or professional support is **not** a sign of weakness; it's a responsible step toward self-betterment.

By **breaking the taboo** around mental health, we encourage honest conversations and seeking help when needed. This fosters a community where **care** and **understanding** become the default responses to emotional struggles. Remember, even the toughest phases will pass, so keep nurturing your mind and soul.

Life Challenges

This activity is especially helpful if you're dealing with:

- **Social Stigma** (Fear of judgment for seeking therapy)

- **Isolation** (Struggling to talk about your feelings)

- **Need for Support Network** (Lacking people to confide in)

Take Care—Your Mental Well-Being Matters

Therapy, professional help, and leaning on your support system are not just safe options; they're **empowering** choices. Just as we see doctors for physical ailments, taking care of mental health is an essential part of overall well-being. Remember: **nothing is permanent**—tough times will eventually yield to better days.

Activity: Connect & Reflect

1. **Identify Three People**

   - List **three individuals** in your life you can talk to openly—friends, family, or a mental health professional.

   - Note **why** each person is someone you trust or find supportive.

2. **Schedule a Chat**

   - Make **one small plan** this week to connect with at least one of these three people.

   - It could be a simple phone call, a coffee meetup, or a casual walk together.

3. **Discuss One Challenge**

   - When you talk, **openly share** one mental or emotional challenge you've been facing.

- Ask for their insights or simply request a listening ear—sometimes, just talking helps.

4. **Reflect on the Conversation**

- Afterward, write down **how you felt** before, during, and after the discussion.

- Did talking relieve any stress or help you see solutions more clearly?

5. **Consider Professional Help**

- If you feel your challenges are overwhelming, **explore therapy** or counseling.

- Write any concerns about therapy (e.g., stigma, cost, uncertainty) and then note potential benefits (e.g., expert guidance, coping strategies, support).

A Positive Note to End On

Stay aware of your mental well-being, talk to people who genuinely matter, and **accept** that therapy is a **positive option**. By treating your mind with the same care you'd give your body, you set the stage for a **healthier, happier, and more resilient life**.

Closing Thoughts:
Beyond the Pitara

Mind Aid Pitara has been an invitation to unmask the illusions we hold within our own minds. Through reflections, practices, and gentle guidance, you've explored the inner landscapes of emotions, resilience, and self-awareness.

The quest doesn't end here. Healing and growth are ongoing processes—each day offers another chance to deepen your insight, strengthen your emotional core, and cultivate compassion for yourself and others. Remember: *nothing is permanent*, and even the toughest chapters will yield to new beginnings.

Above all, guard your mental well-being as a precious resource. Seek professional help if needed—there is no shame in reaching out; in fact, it is an act of courage and self-respect. Share your experiences, confide in those who truly matter, and remind yourself daily that therapy is not a taboo but a step toward wholeness.

Thank you for allowing *Mind Aid Pitara* to be part of your journey. May you continue to unlearn myths—about society, about mental health, and about yourself. Embrace the freedom that comes with dismantling these illusions. Live fully, speak kindly (especially to yourself), and keep your inner flame of hope and curiosity burning bright.

In gratitude and solidarity,

Dr Smita Kamat Ghosh
Author of *Decoding Mithya* and *Mind Aid Pitara*

Glossary

1. **Affirmations**

    Short, positive statements repeated regularly to challenge and overcome negative thoughts or self-sabotaging beliefs.

2. **Anxiety**

    A feeling of worry, nervousness, or unease about an event or an uncertain outcome. It can be mild or severe, sometimes leading to physical symptoms like increased heart rate or sweating.

3. **Cognitive Distortions**

    Faulty or biased ways of thinking that reinforce negative beliefs and emotions. Examples include "all-or-nothing thinking" or "catastrophizing."

4. **Emotional Quotient (EQ)**

    A measure of a person's ability to recognize, understand, manage, and use emotions effectively. High EQ often correlates with better interpersonal relationships and resilience.

5. **Mindfulness**

   A mental state achieved by focusing one's awareness on the present moment, while calmly acknowledging and accepting feelings, thoughts, and bodily sensations.

6. **Positive Psychology**

   A branch of psychology focusing on the strengths and virtues that help individuals and communities thrive, rather than on deficits or mental illness.

7. **Self-Awareness**

   Conscious knowledge of one's own feelings, motives, and desires. It's a key component of emotional intelligence and personal growth.

8. **Self-Care**

   The practice of taking action to preserve or improve one's own health, well-being, and happiness, especially during periods of stress.

9. **Sleep Hygiene**

   Habits and practices that are conducive to sleeping well on a regular basis—such as maintaining a consistent sleep schedule and avoiding caffeine before bedtime.

10. **Stress**

    The body's response to any demand or challenge. It can be positive (eustress) or negative (distress), impacting both physical and mental health.

11. **Stress Management**

Techniques and strategies used to control one's stress levels, including relaxation exercises, time management, and mindfulness practices.

12. **Therapy (Psychotherapy)**

A range of techniques and approaches used by mental health professionals to help individuals understand their feelings, heal from trauma, or work through personal challenges.

13. **Emotional Intelligence (EI)**

The ability to identify, evaluate, control, and express emotions effectively, in oneself and in relationships with others.

14. **Self-Talk**

The internal dialogue that influences how we perceive ourselves and the world around us. It can be positive and encouraging or negative and self-defeating.

15. **Resilience**

The capacity to recover quickly from difficulties or adapt in the face of adversity, stress, or trauma.

Frequently Asked Questions (FAQ)

1. **Q: How do I know if I need professional help instead of just self-help?**
   A: If your emotional struggles, anxiety, or stress begin to significantly interfere with your daily life—such as impacting sleep, work, or relationships—it might be time to consider speaking with a mental health professional. Listening to your mind and body, and seeking help sooner rather than later, is a proactive step toward recovery.

2. **Q: What if I don't have time for self-care routines?**
   A: Self-care doesn't need to be time-consuming. Even small acts—like taking three deep breaths before starting your day, enjoying a quiet cup of tea, or journaling for five minutes—can make a difference. The key is consistency, not quantity.

3. **Q: Can affirmations really help with negative self-talk?**
   A: Yes, affirmations can gradually shift your mindset by replacing negative thoughts with positive, empowering statements. Repetition and consistency are crucial. Over time, these new thought patterns can reshape how you perceive yourself and your challenges.

4. **Q: What if I feel skeptical about mindfulness or meditation?**
   A: It's natural to be skeptical, especially if you're new to mindfulness. Try starting with just a few minutes a day. Experiment with different techniques—guided meditation apps, breathing exercises, or nature walks—to find what resonates with you.

5. **Q: How do I maintain healthy boundaries without feeling guilty?**
   A: Boundaries protect your well-being. It's normal to feel a twinge of guilt when first saying "no" or limiting others' access to your

time and energy. Remember that healthy boundaries are an act of self-respect and ultimately improve relationships by preventing resentment and burnout.

6. **Q: Is it normal to still feel anxious or upset even after following these tips?**

   A: Absolutely. Emotional well-being is an ongoing process, and everyone experiences ups and downs. If difficult emotions persist or intensify, consider reaching out to a counselor, therapist, or mental health hotline for additional support.

7. **Q: Do I have to share my mental health journey with friends or family?**

   A: That choice is entirely yours. While sharing can offer additional support and understanding, it's important to respect your comfort level and privacy. A mental health professional can also provide guidance on how and when to share.

8. **Q: Can I mix these techniques with other self-help or therapy programs?**

   A: Yes. Many people find that combining self-help tools with professional therapy or other programs enriches their journey toward better mental health. Always discuss any concerns with your healthcare professional to ensure approaches align with your needs.

9. **Q: How can I stay motivated to follow these practices long-term?**

   A: Set realistic goals and celebrate small successes. It might help to keep a journal, track your progress, and revisit what you've written when you need a motivational boost. If you feel your enthusiasm wavering, consider enlisting an accountability partner—a friend, family member, or counselor.

10. **Q: How do I know if I need professional therapy instead of self-help?**

    A: If you find persistent emotional distress affecting your ability to function—interrupting sleep, relationships, work, or studies—then seeking professional guidance may help you overcome these challenges more effectively than self-help alone.

11. **Q: What if I'm nervous about my first therapy session?**

    A: It's normal to feel uncertain. A therapist's role is to create a safe, non-judgmental space. They'll guide you step by step, and you can discuss any concerns right at the beginning.

12. **Q: Does therapy mean I'm weak or can't handle life on my own?**

    A: Absolutely not. Therapy is a proactive step toward self-improvement and well-being. Just like consulting a doctor for a physical ailment, reaching out for mental health support is an act of self-care and strength.

13. **Q: How do I pick the right therapist?**

    A: Consider practical factors like specialty, location, and affordability. Arrange a brief phone consultation to see if their approach feels like a good fit. You can always try a different therapist if the first one doesn't meet your needs.

14. **Q: What if I can't afford therapy or don't have insurance?**

    A: Many communities offer low-cost or sliding-scale fees. Some charities and mental health organizations also provide free or subsidized services. Online platforms may also have affordable options.

15. **Q: Is online therapy as effective as in-person sessions?**

    A: Studies indicate that online therapy can be highly effective for many conditions. It offers greater flexibility in scheduling and reduces travel time. However, personal comfort varies—choose whichever setting helps you feel most at ease.

16. **Q: Will therapy solve my problems immediately?**

    A: Therapeutic progress varies from person to person. Change often requires consistent effort both in and out of sessions. Patience and open-mindedness are key to lasting improvement.

17. **Q: How do I maintain therapy benefits after finishing?**

    A: Keep using the tools, exercises, and coping strategies you learned. Continue journaling, practicing mindfulness, or engaging in regular check-ins with a support system. You can always revisit therapy in the future if needed.

Closing Thoughts: Stepping Forward With Wisdom

"The secret of health for both mind and body is not to mourn for the past, not to worry about the future, or not to anticipate troubles, but to live in the present moment wisely and earnestly."

— ***Buddhist Teaching***

"You have the right to work, but never to the fruit of the work. You should never engage in action for the sake of reward, nor should you long for inaction."

— ***Bhagavad Gita***

Embrace the Present

Buddhism reminds us that dwelling in the past or fixating on the future can rob us of the joy and peace found in the here and now. Cultivate mindfulness, allowing each moment to be a new beginning rather than a continuation of old worries.

Act Without Attachment

The Bhagavad Gita teaches us to work wholeheartedly but detach from the outcome. Invest your best efforts; let go of anxiety over results. This practice doesn't lessen your passion—it lightens your burdens.

Foster Compassion and Self-Kindness

In times of struggle, remember these teachings aren't solely about personal gain but also about compassion—for yourself and others. Gentleness in thought, word, and action will nurture your emotional well-being and create ripples of positivity in your relationships.

Find Comfort in Impermanence

Both Buddhist philosophy and the Gita emphasize that nothing is truly permanent—neither pain nor pleasure. This realization can bring hope in hardship and humility in triumph.

Continue the Journey

Through the pages of *Mind Aid Pitara*, you've explored practical tools and reflections to enhance your mental well-being. This is not the end. Use these spiritual insights as anchors in life's storms. Keep learning, keep practicing, and remember that growth is a continual process.

A Last Word of Encouragement

- Believe in Your Potential: Each step you take, no matter how small, is significant.

- Embrace Support: Seek help when needed—be it from friends, family, or professionals—and never see it as weakness.

- Create Hope: Let your determination shape your future, not your doubts.

With gratitude for your commitment to self-discovery, may you find peace, clarity, and enduring strength on your path.

Dr Smita Kamat Ghosh

Author of *Decoding Mithya* and *Mind Aid Pitara*